Ends and Means i

John Kleinig

Routledge
Taylor & Francis Group
LONDON AND NEW YORK

First published 2019 by Routledge

2 Park Square, Milton Park, Abingdon, Oxon OX14 4RN
605 Third Avenue, New York, NY 10017

Routledge is an imprint of the Taylor & Francis Group, an informa business

First issued in paperback 2021

Publisher's Note

The publisher has gone to great lengths to ensure the quality of this reprint but points out that some imperfections in the original copies may be apparent.

Library of Congress Cataloging-in-Publication Data
Names: Kleinig, John, 1942– author.
Title: Ends and means in policing / John Kleinig.
Description: Abingdon, Oxon ; New York, NY : Routledge, 2019. |
Includes index.
Identifiers: LCCN 2018049500 (print) | LCCN 2018051452 (ebook) |
ISBN 9780367025311 (Ebook) | ISBN 9780367025281 (hardback)
Subjects: LCSH: Police ethics. | Ends and means. | Police—Philosophy.
Classification: LCC HV7924 (ebook) | LCC HV7924 .K549 2019 (print) |
DDC 174/.93632—dc23
LC record available at https://lccn.loc.gov/2018049500

ISBN: 978-0-367-02528-1 (hbk)
ISBN: 978-0-367-53016-7 (pbk)

Typeset in Bembo
by Apex CoVantage, LLC

MIX
Paper from responsible sources
FSC www.fsc.org FSC™ C013985

Printed in the United Kingdom
by Henry Ling Limited

Contents

Acknowledgments

It often appears as though those who believe that the ends justify the means and those who do not believe that they do possess quite different and even opposing moral sensibilities—corresponding, perhaps, to that seemingly great divide in moral theory between those who place their trust in some form of consequentialism and those who eschew it. Simplistic though it is to render the contrast in that way, it helps to account for a longtime fascination with the ends-means relationship. It has the added attraction of capturing pivotal terms in many theories of practical reason, which cast themselves in terms of the relation of means to ends. It was not until 1990, when I had already begun working on police ethics and encountered Giuliano Pontara's doctoral dissertation *Does the End Justify the Means? A Metaethical and Normative Study*[1] that the idea of linking a discussion of police ethics with an exploration of the dialectic of ends and means began to take some shape. At that time, formal discussions of police ethics were in their infancy and, apart from Pontara's dissertation, which was now somewhat dated and never published, the ends-means dialectic was often dealt with somewhat peremptorily or by philosophers such as Dewey, who had become unfashionable in the circles in which I moved.

But other projects intervened, and though some of them lent themselves to a treatment that would have involved the means-ends controversy, the thought of bringing the two together was placed on a back burner. Other projects completed, I now have the opportunity to engage in a more synthetic assignment. That said, a good deal of what I may originally have wished to include in a book on ends and means in policing was incorporated in an earlier book, *The Ethics of Policing* (1996). In certain respects, the current volume is to be seen as a follow-up to that earlier one, albeit through a distinctive lens, and in the present volume I have often traveled lightly over issues and examples that were dealt with at greater length in the earlier one.

Although I had originally hoped to draft and test the materials as part of a doctoral course, that was not to be. I am grateful to the (sadly, now defunct) Centre for Applied Philosophy and Public Ethics, Charles Sturt University, for providing some of the initial the conditions for bringing the materials together as well as a philosophical sounding board for some of these materials. Since 2015, I have worked on the materials independently. My wife, Tziporah Kasachkoff, has brought her own editorial and philosophical skills to bear on the evolving manuscript; she has, in the words of the old mower advertisement, transformed "grass into lawn"—and done a fair bit of weeding, as well. Everything is much better as a consequence of her critical eye. Robin Christiaan van Halderen kindly commented on Chapter 10.

In writing this book, I have drawn upon (and frequently revised material from) a number of earlier publications, including *The Ethics of Policing* (New York: Cambridge University Press, 1996); "Noble Cause Corruption or Process Deviance: Ruminations on Means and Ends in Policing," in *Uncertainty, Vol. 4: Police Corruption, Paradigms, Models and Concepts*, eds. Stanley Einstein and Menachem Amir (Huntsville, TX: OICJ Press, 2004), 129–46; "Torture and Political Morality," in *Politics and Morality*, ed. Igor Primoratz (Basingstoke: Palgrave Macmillan, 2007), 209–27; *Ethics and Criminal Justice: An Introduction* (Cambridge, UK: Cambridge University Press, 2008); "Ticking Bombs and Torture Warrants," *Deakin Law Review* 10, no. 2 (2005): 614–27; "Legitimate and Illegitimate Uses of Police Force," *Criminal Justice Ethics* 33, no. 2 (2014): 83–103; "Punishment and the Ends of Policing," in *Liberal Criminal Theory: Essays for Andreas von Hirsch*, ed. A.P. Simester and A. Du Bois-Pedain (Oxford: Hart, 2014), 283–303; and "Trust and Critical Thinking," *Educational Philosophy and Theory* 50, no. 2 (2017): 133–43.

I am grateful for permission to make use of them here.

Note

1. Filosofiska Studier, Häfte 20 (Stockholm: Filosofiska Institutionen vid Stockholms Universitet, 1967).

Introduction

> The end never justifies the means, it is the means which determine what the end will be.[1]

> If the ends don't justify the means, I don't know what will.[2]

Policing is a pragmatic occupation. As an occupational choice, it has been instituted to serve a range of social needs or ends. What those ends are or may legitimately be is a matter of some dispute, though an early account is provided in the 1829 *General Instructions* for the London Metropolitan Police, in which it is stated that the chief end of policing is the "prevention of crime."[3] Other accounts characterize policing as "law enforcement," "the provision of public safety," or even appeal to the overbroad slogan "to serve and protect." Although not identical characterizations, they point in somewhat the same direction. To what extent are these diverse putative ends of policing legitimate and adequate and, qua ends, what constraints need to be placed on them? In seeking to realize them, what means may be employed and under what conditions?

These are the fairly basic but concrete questions from which this study begins. Such questions are, however, particular applications of a more general set of questions about the relationship of means to ends, questions that conceal issues of great complexity. We get some hint of that complexity in the fact that two contrasting assertions—"The ends justify the means" and "The ends never justify the means"—both lay claim to distinguished pedigrees. Given that such assertions are boldly put forward by their respective protagonists, especially in the realms of social policy and political strategy, we might expect that something can be said for each, and that the truth lies somewhere between them or perhaps somewhere else.

What follows is an attempt to explore the complex relationships between ends and means, especially insofar as the issue of justification is concerned and to illustrate some of that more abstract discussion with examples that are most often drawn from the criminal justice domain, particularly policing.

In the remainder of these introductory remarks, I will provide an overview of some of the general contours of the means-end relation, noting salient issues and how they impact on policing. That will then set the scene for the chapters that follow.

In practical reasoning, the means-end relation is ubiquitous, even if not exhaustive.[4] In order to assuage my thirst, I drink water. I have a desire to render public service, and so I join the police force. A person is deemed to be socially dangerous, and is therefore taken into custody and perhaps imprisoned. My drain is blocked, and I call a plumber to fix it. I rob a bank in order to pay my debts. I want my children to share my religious beliefs, so I make them go to church.

In each of these cases, an "end" can be posited—removal of thirst, rendering public service, securing public order and safety, unblocking a drain, payment of debts, and having one's children accept one's religious beliefs—and a "means" is employed to achieve that end—respectively, drinking water, joining a police service, arresting and imprisoning a dangerous person, calling a plumber, robbing a bank, and requiring that one's children go to church.

Reflection on such means-end statements generates a range of issues. For example, there is the matter of what we might term the "causal efficacy" or, even more generally, "causal appropriateness" of the means—whether the means employed are causally appropriate to the end (that is, could bring it about) or are likely to, or will actually bring it about or achieve it. Certain assumptions may be implicit in statements about the means. For example, we need to presume that the water I drink is not salty or that the thirst is not caused by some medical condition that water is unable to alleviate. In the case of joining the police, the assumption is not only that policing constitutes a public service, but that the particular police department I join is not a rogue one. Merely calling a plumber to unblock a drain will not unblock it—the plumber must come and be capable of dealing with the block. And so on.

In addition, there will be issues about the *legitimacy* and *adequacy* of ends.[5] Public service seems to be innocent enough—indeed, quite admirable—but that is probably because we presume, conventionally, that the public to be served shares broadly liberal democratic values. But joining the German police force during the years of National Socialism may have served public ends of a significantly unacceptable kind. What public is being served? Even if it represents a majority, it may be an oppressive or acquiescent one. Even in liberal democratic societies, such as the United States, questions have been raised about whether its policing institutions are irremediably racist and inegalitarian and in need of abolition.[6]

Unblocking a drain may seem to be innocuous enough, because we presume that the drain is removing undesirable waste. But, to recast a metaphor, if, when the drain is unblocked, the baby will disappear along with the bathwater, we may have second thoughts.[7] More generally, how, if at all, can we determine the legitimacy and adequacy of ends?

There will, further, be independent questions about the "legitimacy of means." Assuming that debts are not generally good to have or to have too long, is it legitimate to deal with them by robbing a bank (even assuming that this will enable the debts to be paid)? And we may well wonder whether making children go to church constitutes a legitimate—or even effective—means for getting them to share one's religious faith, presuming, controversially, that such an end is legitimate.

The assumption in some of these cases is that the end in question will "justify" the particular means used. That is, not only will the means be adequate to bringing about the end, but also that use of the means in question will be legitimate. What, however, is it for means to be justified? Is the end ever sufficient to justify the means, or do the means have to pass muster on their own? Are there other constraints? Must the means be efficacious or, given the circumstances, simply probable? That is, is justification ex ante or ex post? If the means fail to produce the end, was their employment therefore unjustified? And if unjustified, does that represent a moral failure on the part of the user? Or is it enough that the means were sincerely (and reasonably?) believed to secure the end for which they were intended? Is there, perhaps, a more intimate connection between ends and means such that, as some have suggested, the means determine what the end will be?

As should be clear, there are many assumptions behind and questions raised by means-end talk, and it will be our task in what follows to expose some of them and seek to respond to them.

* * *

The issue of ends and means—whether ends justify means and whether some means are unjustified regardless of the ends to which they are directed—is as old as the use of practical reasoning and moral reflection. In Genesis, Abraham is visited by God and told that, for their wickedness, the inhabitants of Sodom and Gomorrah will be destroyed (Genesis 18, 19). Abraham does not dispute the judgment about the general character of the inhabitants of the cities, but takes issue with the means. "Shall not the judge of all the earth do right?" he asks. "What if there are 50 righteous people there? Would you destroy the innocent along with the wicked?" God indicates that if his proposed means would result in the death of 50 righteous people, he would not do what he proposed. Abraham continues to argue, progressively lowering the numbers, seeking assurances that the destruction of the cities will not involve means that are destructive of the innocent.[8]

For reference to a modern debate, we can turn to discussions about the use of intrusive surveillance, detention, torture, and "enhanced interrogation techniques" to combat terrorism. Does a larger social purpose—whether the visitation of retributive justice or the guarding of public safety—justify the use of means that are morally problematic, and if, in certain circumstances, it does, what parameters are to be observed? Abraham's intercession on behalf of the innocent in Sodom and Gomorrah led to the "rescue" of Lot and his family. And some, desirous of avoiding the use of torture, have nevertheless proposed harsh interrogatory measures that are said to be less than torture—in the parlance of some, "torture-lite."[9]

The Sodom and Gomorrah story is not so much about public safety as it is about punishment—punishment as an end—and the means that might be employed to achieve that end. But should punishment be imposed as an end, or simply as a means to some further end, such as justice, societal purity, rehabilitation, or public safety? Is it, in the language of Aristotle, an intermediate or final end? Might intermediate ends be appealed to in justification of particular means, and if not, what are the characteristics of a final end? May final ends themselves be means? Are there some means—such as deliberately killing the innocent—that are impermissible no matter what the end? Or are some ends so important that any means may be used to achieve them?

When it is asked whether the ends justify the means that are used to bring them about, it is tempting to think of means and ends as discrete categories. We shall question that separation. The point is not that there is no distinction to be drawn, but that drawing the distinction in certain ways can be problematic. For not only may particular ends themselves be means (to further ends)—what Aristotle considered a hierarchy of ends[10]—but the means that are used to bring them about may also be determinative of their achievement. To go back to an earlier example, if religious faith is considered to involve a free acceptance of certain beliefs or voluntarily entering into a certain commitment, then seeking to bring it about by forcible means may subvert the end's realization.

* * *

In investigating the various issues and questions raised, we will adopt the following broad strategy. First of all, we will look at the idea of an end, tracing the various ways in which ends may be construed, and highlighting those understandings that underlie means-end justifications. This will lead into a discussion of the ends of policing. Then we will engage in a similar exploration of means. Given that the central question at issue is one of justification, we will then move to a discussion of what we may understand by, and expect of, a justification, and the conditions under which ends might be thought to justify the employment of particular means. Again, we will give general consideration to the use of means in policing. This will constitute the theoretical heart of the study.

In the latter chapters, we will move to a series of increasingly concrete issues, focusing especially on those that arise in policing contexts. The first challenge will be to consider the implications of a protracted debate about the bearing that intentions may have on the legitimacy of certain otherwise problematic means. Well-known in the medical ethics literature as the Doctrine of Double Effect (DDE), it may also be invoked in the context of police ethics.[11] Our next task will be to engage with a view most famously associated with Kant; namely, that people are to be treated as ends and not merely as means. What does this mean? Is it plausible? How does it impinge on practice, and on policing in particular? The following chapter will explore the issue of problematic and impermissible means: are there some means whose use can never enter into a justification, no matter what the ends? Or: may any means be justified, depending on the circumstances? Here we will give some attention to the issue of torture—often presented as impermissible, no matter what—and the relevance of the so-called ticking bomb argument to that view. But we will also touch on what might be argued to be contingently impermissible means. For example, closely related to the issue of torture, we will review the use of third-degree tactics, and then some of the challenges posed by the use of sexual tactics as an investigative tool, as well as the controversy caused by the recent US Supreme Court decision to permit strip searches whenever an arrested person is about to be jailed. Inter alia, these will require that we engage with matters of proportionality.

Some means, though not morally impermissible, nevertheless raise serious moral concerns. Here we will consider the use of various surveillance, data mining, and profiling technologies, and the challenges they pose for the safeguarding of privacy, autonomy, integrity, and dignity. These are not, of course, the only means that raise serious moral concerns. As well as the deception and manipulation that is often involved in policing techniques, police work is closely associated with the use of coercive force, and we will need to confront its appropriate limits. Our primary concern in this chapter will be with the effects of using particular means on the public trust that is central to police work.

The competing moral demands made by ends and means is sometimes said to create "dirty hands" situations; that is, ones in which, even if the use of a certain means to secure a particular end is justified, the person who employs or authorizes those means is left with (morally) dirty hands. Can we give a morally coherent account of dirty hands, or does their recognition involve an unacceptable moral compromise? This will lead naturally into a discussion of what has come to be known in policing as noble cause corruption, sometimes characterized by reference to dirty hands theory (but also amenable to other interpretations). In all these cases, the dialectic of means and ends is foregrounded, though each is also likely to involve other considerations.

Notes

1. Sometimes attributed to Mahatma Gandhi. See, for possible sources, Raghawan N. Iyer, "Means and Ends in Politics," in *Gandhi: His Relevance for Our Times*, ed. G. Ramachandran and T.K. Mahadevan, 2nd ed. (New Delhi: Kapur Printing Press/Gandhi Peace Foundation, 1971), available at: www.mkgandhi.org/g_relevance/chap28.htm. Similar statements are found in Aldous Huxley: "The end cannot justify the means for the simple and obvious reason that the means employed determine the nature of the

end produced," *Ends and Means: An Enquiry into the Nature of Ideals and into the Methods Employed for Their Realization* (London: Chatto & Windus, 1937), 10; cf. also 52: "the means inevitably determine the nature of the result achieved"; and Ralph Waldo Emerson: "the end pre-exists in the means, the fruit in the seed," "Compensation," in *The Essays of Emerson*, Vol. 1 (London: A.L. Humphreys, 1899), 111.

2. Attributed to Woody Allen. See also note 9.
3. Metropolitan Police, *Instructions to Police Officers* (London: HMSO, 1829), 1; cf. 20, 47. In saying that the prevention of crime is policing's chief end, the implication was that it also had other ends. See later.
4. Some, indeed, consider that means-end thinking distorts practical reasoning by simplifying what we are doing when we reason practically. Here I say only that it is a part of practical reasoning.
5. In these introductory remarks, I avoid some of the questions that might be asked about "legitimacy"—whether it is institutional, ethical, moral, political, normative. And I do not make distinctions among the latter that might be made. Ultimately, my concern is with moral legitimacy, though, given the contextual concern with criminal justice, it might be characterizable as ethical legitimacy. Also, I do not here presume a particular relationship between, say, political and moral legitimacy. Later on, where distinctions seem appropriate, I will make them.
6. See, e.g., Mychal Denzel Smith, "Abolish the Police: Instead, Let's Have Full Social, Economic, and Political Equality," *The Nation*, 4/9/2015, available at: www.thenation.com/article/abolish-police-instead-lets-have-full-social-economic-and-political-equality/. A judgment to similar effect was made in Northern Ireland when the Royal Ulster Constabulary (RUC) was closed down in 2001, and then reconstituted as the Police Service of Northern Ireland (PSNI) under The Police (Northern Ireland) Act 2000, available at: www.legislation.gov.uk/ukpga/2000/32/contents/enacted.
7. Compare the old joke: "The operation was successful, but the patient died."
8. As for the actual phrase, "the end justifies the means" (and its equivalents), there are various Latin precursors: *Cui licitus est finis, etiam licent media; cum finis est licitus, etiam media sunt licita; finis sanctificat media*. Ovid also writes: *exitus acta probat* (outcomes justify actions), in *The Heroides*, II.85, available at: http://poetryintranslation.com/PITBR/Latin/Heroides1-7.htm#_Toc523806686. St. Jerome cites the formula in *Letter* 48, para 14, referring negatively to "the line—so often adopted by strong men in controversy—of justifying the means by the result," available at: www.ccel.org/ccel/schaff/npnf206.v.XLVIII.html; cf. also Matthew Prior (1664–1721), *Hans Carvel*: "The End must justifie the Means," available at: www.poetry-archive.com/p/hans_carvel.html. Some link the doctrine, if not the exact phrase, to Niccolò Machiavelli who, though he comes close to it, does not use the exact phrase: "It is well then, when the deed accuses him, the result should excuse him," *Discourses on Livy*, II. 9, available at: https://ebooks.adelaide.edu.au/m/machiavelli/niccolo/m149d/book1.html#book1.9; "I think not according to your perspective, wherein nothing but prudence is visible, but to the perspective of the many, which must see the ends, not the means, of things," letter to Giovan Battista Soderini, from *Machiavelli and His Friends: Their Personal Correspondence* (DeKalb, IL: Northern Illinois University Press, 1996), 134–6, available at: www2.idehist.uu.se/distans/ilmh/Ren/flor-mach-ghiribizzi.htm.
9. Jessica Wolfendale, "The Myth of 'Torture Lite'," *Ethics & International Affairs* 23, no. 1 (2009): 47–61.
10. See Aristotle, *Nicomachean Ethics*, bk. 1, ch. 1, §1094a.
11. See, e.g., Vidar Halvorsen's unpublished doctoral dissertation, *Ethics, Force and Violence in Policing* (University of Oslo, Acta Humaniora, 2001).

Chapter 1

Ends

> Every sort of expert knowledge and every inquiry, and similarly every action and undertaking, seems to seek some good. Because of that, people are right to affirm that "the good is that which all things seek." But there appears to be a certain difference among ends: some are activities, while others are products of some kind over and above the activities themselves. Where there are ends over and above the activities, in these cases the products are by nature better than the activities.[1]

> We deliberate not about ends but about means. For a doctor does not deliberate whether he shall heal, nor an orator whether he shall persuade, nor a statesman whether he shall produce law and order, nor does anyone else deliberate about his end. They assume the end and consider how and by what means it is to be attained; and if it seems to be produced by several means they consider by which it is most easily and best produced, while if it is achieved by one only they consider how it will be achieved by this and by what means this will be achieved, till they come to the first cause, which in the order of discovery is last.[2]

As evidenced by these quotations from Aristotle, there is a long history to the consideration of ends. Aristotle figures in much of that history. He views ends as the true objects of action, and suggests that, despite their multiplicity, the ends of acts are ultimately characterizable as "the good" at which we aim. Ends may be activities or some product of activity. Where they are the latter, they take precedence over the former. Somewhat surprisingly, in the second quotation he suggests that ends are not themselves objects of deliberation—only means are, and we deliberate about them in order to judge their efficiency and acceptability.

Our discussion of ends will not be an exercise in Aristotelian scholarship, though it is useful to see the variety of issues that Aristotle raises, while making only a brief reference to the means that are employed to achieve them. I do not mean to underplay the importance of means and of considering ends and means together, but intend rather to emphasize that ends raise issues in their own right and not only because of their place in the means-ends relation.

Although, as the quotations indicate, the idea of an end is central to Aristotle's account of practical reasoning, it also plays an important role in his larger scheme of things. That larger scheme is often referred to as teleological: the view that natural/living as well as artifactual objects possess ends (*téle*)—something toward which they tend—as part of the kinds of things that they are. According to this view, almond trees will tend toward producing flowers and nuts; zebras will tend toward maturity and reproductive activity; and a grub's end will be turning into a butterfly that lays eggs. For Aristotle, the realization of these things' ends constitutes the flourishing of those things. In the case of man-made artifacts such as musical instruments or knives, they will have as their ends the purpose for which they were made (music or cutting), and good instances of each will be those that, respectively, produce good sounds or cut well. For Aristotle, humans also have ends; humans have, moreover, an ultimate end—what Aristotle calls *eudaimonia* (sometimes translated as "happiness," but better thought of as "living well").[3]

Although supporters of (some version of) Aristotelian teleology can still be found, teleology as a general theory of things does not have a great deal of contemporary support. Even if it makes sense to speak of natural objects—such as trees—as "flourishing," this need not be understood in terms of fulfilling their natural ends (*téle*). The language of ends is more appropriately understood as one that we use in relation either to human action of some kind or to the intentional products of human action, such as musical instruments or knives.[4] The reason for this is that, typically, human action is purposive, whether we act individually, collectively, or through various institutions or other social artifacts and structures. It is not that Aristotle had a somewhat animistic view of living natural objects, attributing to them purposes or intentions, but that what he saw as ends (embodied in flourishing) might now be accounted for in other ways (e.g., as the result of evolutionary processes). In any case, the attribution of ends to natural objects such as trees, though grounded in their actual features, is something that we—as humans—attribute to them as one of the ways in which we make sense of the world to ourselves.

The language of "ends" is not the only one we might use, and sometimes its use may even sound a bit archaic or stilted. Sometimes we may prefer to talk instead of aims, goals, ambitions, purposes, intentions, aspirations, desired results, targets, motivating ideas, or objectives.[5] Sometimes, but not always. No doubt, there are nuances to the language of ends that are not present when we adopt the terminology of, say, aims or goals. Certainly, when the talk is of *justifying* means by reference to the ends they are designed to realize, or when we talk of the distinction between intermediate and final ends, the vocabulary of ends seems most apt—and not only most apt, but also as having a normative dimension. We see ends, and certainly final, terminal, or ultimate ends as "ends in themselves" or as things sought for their own sake, or that are valued or valuable, and the means as (in part or

Even if it can be argued that there are ends toward which we or other living organisms are directed or "tend," it might be questioned whether they are predetermined and unchanging. Might such ends be fluid and contingent on shifting circumstances rather than somehow fixed in nature? The philosopher John Dewey expended a good deal of ink in relativizing both means and ends to circumstances.[8] And perhaps they may be relativized to subjects, as well. What Alfred treats as a means may be an end for Bruce, or what at one time Bruce treats as an end he may at another time come to see as only a means. Say, Alfred sees political power as a means to social reform whereas Bruce values power for its own sake. Or imagine that Bruce enters on a law career hoping to make lots of money and retire at 40, but discovers by the time he has reached 40 that he now finds fulfillment in legal pursuits—and so his legal career has now become an end in itself.[9] What initially attracts a person to law enforcement may be its adventurous possibilities, along with generous employment benefits. After a while, however, the job becomes part of her life and identity, and she continues in it for its own sake. This suggests that there may not be a fixed order of means and ends.

What the previous suggests is that we may conceive of final or ultimate ends either as relative to particular circumstances or as something inherent in the nature of things. It is Dewey's contention that the latter view has led to utopianism, fanaticism, and totalitarianism.[10] For Dewey, people's ends arise for them when their engagement with their environment leads them to experience some lack or deficiency; their ends are constituted by states of affairs whose realization therefore has some claim on them.[11] Those states of affairs lead agents to reflect on what means, from where they are, will lead to their realization—what Dewey refers to as "ends-in-view" (since the means may not actually accomplish them). These, for Dewey, are agents' final or ultimate ends, or at least they are insofar as they achieve some overall coordination of such agents' activities. They are not final, however, in the sense that they bring the agents' activities to some sort of conclusion:

> Ends [in view] are foreseen consequences which arise in the course of activity and which are employed to give activity added meaning and to direct its further course. They are in no sense ends *of* action. In being ends of *deliberation* they are redirecting pivots *in* action.[12]

As Dewey understands it, ends are not "out there," fixed and independent of the experience and activity of the agent. Ends are developed in the course of agential activity in the world, and they may evolve over time.[13] He does not altogether reject the idea that some generalized ends might constitute a framework for thinking about ends-in-view, but even those are subject to review by the agent.

whole) *warranted* by the fact that they are employed to bring about :
Whether there are such normative ends and, if so, what their nat
be, has been a matter of longstanding controversy.[6]

Although ends tend to figure centrally in discussions of pract soning, it is probably misleading to think of such means-end rel: exhausting the domain of practical reasoning.[7] Other models of p reason have employed specification (Henry Richardson) or incor organic or part-whole thinking. Thus, I may eat nutritious foods i to stay healthy, and staying healthy is, for me, an element in my flc ing. But health is not a means to flourishing, so much as a part of i same has often been argued with respect to the relation between and *eudaimonia* (living well). Is the former a means to the latter or, often been argued, a constituent of the latter? But the present proj not intended to exhaust the domain of practical reason, but only to sider that dimension in which ends are linked to means, and usually justificatory purposes.

For Aristotle, the end of action is sought as a good for its own sak either the good associated with a particular sphere of human activity, say— use Aristotle's examples—health as the good aimed at by medicine, or wea as the good aimed at by household management. Or the end of action sought as some overall good for Man (*eudaimonia*). (Aristotle has a hard tin imagining that human activities, along with human organs, could "aim" various goods without Man himself having some good toward which h activities are directed. It is, however, hardly a matter of logic that this should be the case, and we will later have some reason to qualify it.)

Clearly, our having an end is more than our simply having something that we want, wish, or desire—it must be something that that we seek to achieve *as the result of our action*. No doubt, because of certain wants, wishes, or desires, we may come to decide on certain actions that will realize the wants, wishes or desires that we have—either as short- or long-term goals. But that does not reduce such ends to mere wants, etc. The objects of desire do not have to be attainable (though some might argue that they must be believed to be). Even this, however, is arguably too strong: may I have world peace as my end without believing it to be realizable (by me or at all)? There may also be less to an end than something we want, wish, or desire. Sometimes we may be said to have ends without wanting them. If it is said that the end of human life is to glorify God, that may not be something *I* have any wish to do: it may not be *my* end, even if it is claimed to be an end of human life. Or, if I am a police officer, it may be said that the end of police work is public safety, even if, for some, the end of their police work may be not much more than having a secure job with good benefits. The good of a profession may be one thing, though the good sought by some of its members might be otherwise. In certain contexts, these complications may be important (though for the most part I shall ignore them).

Humans undoubtedly have ends when they act purposively. These ends give shape, and ultimately meaning, to what they do. The ends a person has may be immediate or remote, intermediate or final, instrumental or terminal, first or ultimate—to use some of the contrasts that are often drawn between the different ends that we may have. Aristotle himself speaks of a hierarchy of ends in which some ends (intermediate) are pursued to accomplish other ends, and others (final) are pursued for their own sakes. Final ends may themselves be differentiated, on the one hand, into those that, though pursued for their own sakes, also serve as means to further ends, and, on the other hand, ends that can be said to be "most final" (or ultimate), in that they serve no purpose beyond their being realized. I may, for example, get tennis lessons to improve my tennis game, though my playing tennis is enjoyable and so figures for me as an end in itself. Of course, though tennis may be an end in itself I may pursue it as well because it increases my fitness, and my fitness may be an element in my pursuit of a good life (*eudaimonia*).

Part of the significance often attributed to the intermediate/final end distinction is the supposition that final ends are the only kinds of ends that can constitute goods of sufficient importance to sustain the claim that the end justifies the means.[14] The view is that intermediate ends, even if they are pursued as ends in themselves, may not be linked to values of sufficient considerability to justify the means that are intended to secure them.[15] Moreover, not every intermediate end is pursued as an end in itself. Some ends may be merely instrumental. The means employed to open a box may be a screwdriver to loosen the cover or a hammer to break it open. Unless opening the box is represented in a particular way (say, by linking it to goods or by asserting that it is in itself good), the question of whether, in cases such as this, the end *justifies* the means will not normally arise. For in these cases, our ends are simply as the (intended) outcomes or consequences of action. What we aim to bring about may represent what we desire to do, but what we desire to do may not be viewed, even by us, as something worthwhile.

In coming to grips with some of the issues raised so far, it is useful to consider some of the points made by Harry Frankfurt in an influential paper, "On the Usefulness of Final Ends."

Frankfurt prefers to use the language of "instrumental" and "terminal" ends to make Aristotle's distinction between actions that are justifiable as means to some end and those that are deemed either worth pursuing for their own sake or valuable in themselves. The Aristotelian way of making the distinction bothers Frankfurt (we will have more to say about this later) because it imagines a world in which the value of means is exclusively a function of the ends that these means serve. For Frankfurt, a particular means may have a value that is quite independent of the ends it serves: if using the third degree on someone results in getting a confession, that confession, whatever we may think of its reliability, is not what gives the use of the third degree the value that it has. Use of the third degree is morally problematic, *whatever* end it serves.

A further worry that Frankfurt has with Aristotle's account is that whereas Aristotle thinks that *actions* or *activities* can have ends or aims (see the epigraph), Frankfurt wishes to restrict the having of ends to agents. True, we might argue that insofar as actions and activities are engaged in by agents, there is no problem about attributing ends to the former. But Frankfurt wants to keep a firm focus on the intentionality of ends, and intentionality is always agent-based.

Why *are* we end-oriented? The obvious answer is that there are particular ends we want to achieve. I want to slake my thirst, to raise socially responsible children, to finish a degree or project, to stamp out crime, and so forth. But those answers tend to generate another round of questions: why slake my thirst, raise responsible children, finish a degree or particular project, or stamp out crime? We might then answer by positing some further end that these stated ends can be expected to advance. Or we might claim that these ends are things we pursue for their own sakes and not because of any further end that they serve. The initial question, however, is meant to probe rather deeper into our having of ends at all rather than a question about why we have the particular ends that we value.

It is Frankfurt's contention that a life without ends is a life without meaning. I have already hinted at this. We may suffer and benefit without ends, preferring that which benefits us to that which causes us suffering, and our having ends may assist us in avoiding suffering and gaining that which benefits us—that is, assists us more than if we had no ends. But, Frankfurt argues, a life devoid of ends would be a life devoid of meaning. Having ends is what makes for our having a meaningful and meaningfully human life—not, perhaps, any and every end, but some ends.

To say that a life has meaning is to say that it has meaning *for us*. This is not quite the same as saying that it is a meaningful life. A life that is meaningless to its possessor may be meaningful insofar as it illustrates to others the importance of having ends. Or it may have achievements that others appreciate and value, while being of no significance to the person whose achievements they are. And a life that has meaning for its possessor may nevertheless be seen as meaningless from a wider social perspective or in the greater scheme of things. A person may collect bottle tops as his overarching goal in life—this is what gives *his* life meaning—but we may wonder whether, from some "third-person" point of view, such a life could be considered meaningful. Within the larger scheme of human possibilities, such a life would have a Sisyphian pointlessness.[16]

To the extent that Frankfurt is correct about the importance of having ends, and perhaps of having ends that can reasonably be counted as meaningful, then the question of ends is not something we can simply dispense with as an optional human concern, but will be of importance both individually and socially. If we grant this, then the question of how such ends are to be secured—that is, the question of means to employ and to secure these ends—will never be far behind.

For our lives to have meaning (to us), it is not necessary that our lives be happy, or even that our lives be good ones. All that is necessary is that, for us, what our lives are directed to (that is, our ends) is important to us. That, for Frankfurt, is engagement in activities that we care about (whether or not we are successful in accomplishing what we care about). Caring about something—that is, giving it action-guiding importance—is central to Frankfurt's larger philosophical project (which I shall not pursue here).

Let us return to Frankfurt's contention—noted earlier—that there is a distinction to be made between something being a final end and its being good in itself, or intrinsically valuable. The judgment that something counts as a final end for someone is a judgment that that end is pursued or adopted by that person in a certain way—that is, as an end in itself. In contrast, the judgment that something is good in itself is a judgment about the characteristics that that thing is deemed to have, whether or not it is pursued or adopted by anyone. Calling it good in itself or intrinsically valuable simply indicates that the good or value that it is thought to possess is not derivative of the consequences it has or the further ends it serves. It is not to imply that value's timelessness or contextlessness.

For Frankfurt, our final ends should not be determined *solely* by judgments about the goodness of those ends, but rather how pursuit of those ends affects how we live. Suppose that the effort required to achieve a certain end of considerable inherent value is minimal and so a life devoted *solely* to realizing that end would be nearly empty. Something of much lesser inherent value, however, "might require invigoratingly complicated and wholehearted attention."[17] A life devoted to such an end may therefore be full of purpose and in this respect possess meaning. Of course, effort per se does not make what we do meaningful: Sisyphus was condemned to ceaseless and considerable effort, but it was not the kind of effort that added meaning to his life. Indeed, even a life devoted to something more complex and engaging may not be worthwhile in *other* ways.

We noted earlier a distinction between something sought for its own sake and something being good or valuable in itself. It is important to see that this distinction does not imply that the person who seeks something as an end in itself does not *also* value it. Our valuing it says something about ourselves—what we think it is important to pursue—and this is not necessarily a statement about the intrinsic properties we ascribe to what we pursue.

As the title of Frankfurt's essay suggests, having final ends serves a useful purpose in human life. Not only may it be a source of meaning for us, but it also enables our survival as the particular persons we are. A recognizable self cannot exist without final ends to sustain it. Thus, final ends are useful insofar as they are instrumental to our having lives that are meaningful for us. The identification of something as the kind of final end that contributes to a meaningful life is not determinable in a simple linear fashion. It may, for example, be important to the meaning of my life that I am engaged in useful work—I may desire it for its own sake—but that work may be of instrumental value in that it serves some further social purpose. I may, for example, work as a graphic designer, producing artifacts that others will find useful for the pursuit of their ends, but insofar as graphic design is work that I pursue for its own sake, it will not only serve others' ends, but be a final end and thus an element within a meaningful life.

Final ends need not be singular. My life may be bounded by a number of different final ends, and it may be necessary that we play off one end against another. Granted, they may be accommodated under some overall final end such as *eudaimonia*, though it need not be the case that a final end of that kind be directly pursued rather than be seen as the natural outcome of and judgment upon other ends that are pursued.

Deliberating About and Justifying (Final) Ends

What justifies the ends we choose and pursue? Are ends like tastes—*de gustibus non est disputandum* (roughly, in matters of taste, there is no place for argument), such that nothing can be said to justify one against another? Are they left dangling in justificatory space, or can they themselves be subject to *some* form of justification? Can they be deliberated about, and if so, how? Does it matter here whether we're dealing with ends or final ends—such that we might countenance deliberation concerning the former but not the latter?

We will, for now, defer the question of what *justifying* an end might consist of[18]—and focus simply on *deliberation* about what to do. We are here confronted by some deep philosophical disagreements. Some argue that (final) ends are just "given"—things we desire—and are not amenable to rational deliberation and justification, whereas others argue that unless ends themselves can be subject to justificatory scrutiny, the whole enterprise of justification is rendered pointless or at least superficial. It remains suspended in non-rational space. As an example of the former position, Donald Hubin argues that:

> the agent's ultimate ends (I would say, "her intrinsic values") are neither rationally advisable nor rationally inadvisable, in themselves. They are, rather, the brute facts about the agent's psychology in virtue of a relationship to which policies, plans, and actions can be rationally advisable or inadvisable.[19]

The alternative position or, perhaps more accurately, the cluster of alternative positions, is represented by Christine Korsgaard, who argues that:

> Unless there are normative principles directing us to the adoption of certain ends, there can be no requirement to take the means to our ends.[20]

As we noted at the beginning, Aristotle appears to take the former position when he says: "We deliberate not about ends but about means." But his example does not require the conclusion that we *cannot* deliberate about ends.[21] When he says, for example, "a doctor does not deliberate whether he shall heal, . . . nor a statesman whether he shall produce law and order," he may simply be taken to claim that qua doctor or statesman, a doctor or statesman does not deliberate about whether he should heal or produce law and order. But if a person is wondering whether he should be a doctor or statesman, it may well be the case that he deliberates about what his ends should be. And a person who, after such deliberation decides to be a statesman, may later change his mind when he sees the cost to his integrity that being a statesman will involve. I don't think Aristotle rules this out: as noted, he doesn't say that a person cannot deliberate about ends, only that people (or at least role occupants) ordinarily make practical decisions knowing what their ends are and ask what they need to do to realize those ends.

It might even be the case—though Aristotle may not have thought so—that a doctor or statesman could raise questions about the appropriate ends of doctoring or statesmanship: is it, or should it be, healing or producing law and order? Perhaps appeals to the ends of doctoring or statesmanship are not the best approach here, simply because the ends of these occupations may seem rather obvious. But a police officer who could be said to have "enforcing the law" as her end might seriously question whether *that* should constitute the end of what she does. She might wonder whether it is too restrictive and thus distorts the real work of social peacekeeping to which she believes police officers should be devoted. Perhaps she could do more to keep the social peace as a social justice lawyer or politician?

Even an ultimate end may become an object of deliberation. Take, for example, the "most final" end of human life—for Aristotle the claim that Man's final end is *eudaimonia* (living well) as well as the (catechetical) assertion that the chief end of man is "to glorify God, and to enjoy him forever."[22] How might one choose between such assertions? Are these ends commensurable, such that one can make a reasonable choice between them, or is there no rational way of comparing them?[23] One might, of course, seek to collapse them by saying that (for some?) *eudaimonia* may consist in glorifying God. (Such was the contention of Augustine, and later Pascal. In his *Confessions*, Augustine famously wrote: "You have made us for yourself, O Lord, and our hearts are restless until they rest in you.")[24] Of course, that still leaves us with the need to justify the theological claim.

Assume that we can think of one of these two ends as only a particular specification of the other. Do we just intuitively *see* that *eudaimonia* is justified, or as not needing justification? More fundamentally, does the very activity of deliberation presuppose an end in order to get traction, thus making a final end the condition for deliberative reflection? Is *eudaimonia* an end that we non-rationally opt for because it fits with how we see ourselves—perhaps as a result of the early nurture we have received? Or is there some one end—*eudaimonia*—that fits with being human, with certain capacities that (other?) animals might not have? Might we appeal to the Aristotelian idea that ends can be determined by reference to the living object's *flourishing*? And if, as Aristotle suggests, human flourishing is constituted by *eudaimonia*, might that flourishing manifest itself in a variety of ways? May what enables Alice to flourish be quite different from what enables Brian to flourish? If there are different ways in which humans can flourish, is there some common thread that is shared by those who flourish? It was Aristotle's view—though one that has been contested by others—that human flourishing requires (or is partly constituted by) the acquisition of virtue. Even if that is accepted, we may still raise the question of which virtues need to be acquired if humans are to flourish. Different writers focus on different virtues (or catalogues thereof) and it is at least arguable that the different catalogues suggested by different writers are not entirely compatible. What Nietzsche derides as "Christian virtues" or Hume slights as "monkish virtues" may sit awkwardly with other enumerations of the virtues.[25]

There are many questions here, and some of them resurface when we consider not only "most final" ends, but also ends that are more intermediately final—that is, ends that we may value for themselves or see as valuable in themselves, but are less ultimate than *eudaimonia* or the glorification of God. Such ends might be the ends of particular occupations or professions, such as policing or law or medicine or the ends of certain roles such as parenting or teaching. How shall we establish these ends? And how shall we prioritize them should we have to choose among them? If they are amenable to some hierarchy of ends, how do we establish the priority of one over another?

Or, to go back to our previous example of the possibility that *eudaimonia* and "glorifying God and enjoying him forever" represents alternative ultimate ends, how might one resolve a conflict between them? We could examine each of the proffered ultimate ends, unpacking its presumptions and then seeing how well those presumptions stand up to scrutiny. So, *eudaimonia* might be articulated and questioned in a number of ways. Is it constituted by a subjective satisfaction with life, or must it also contain certain elements such as a life of virtue? Might it be something that one can gain or lose over time, or should we accept the Solonic view that *ending* life well is of critical importance to judging someone "happy"? The theologically structured ultimate end invites questions about the identity and existence of such a being as God. Of course, the same kind of process might be instituted, no matter what the ultimate end is taken to be.

* * *

Disputes about ends and final ends may arise in at least three different ways. There can be disagreements among people whether *all* purposive activities—even, perhaps, games and sporting activities—have an end, and about what the end of some particular activity might be. Is the end of policing social order, law enforcement, crisis management, or something else? And how shall we prioritize or resolve clashes among ends (say, between ambitions as a police officer and the desire to be a good parent or spouse)?

The task of establishing or defending final and ultimate ends is a daunting one, and it may not be one that can be done once and for all. There are very few claims about ends (or even propositions more generally) that do not give rise to justificatory questions, and the justifications we give may be inherently provisional. (More on that later.) In some cases, it may be possible to call putative final ends into question because they are embedded in metaphysical structures that are deemed to be problematic, if not deeply confused or mistaken. As we just noted, the view that it is the end of man to "glorify God and enjoy him forever" presumes, first, that there is a God; and, second, that if there is, God has made Man for a certain purpose, both contestable claims. Even more modest presumptions, such as that *eudaimonia* is the final end of Man, may be thought to rely on a particular view of human nature that is difficult to agree about, let alone establish.

Conclusion

There is some reason to think that what we call ends figure centrally in human activity and experience. Ends are action-guiding in the sense that they provide a reason for doing something. It is also the having of ends that gives meaning to human experience: without ends, we have no way of centering our lives. In saying that, however, I do not want to insist that there is, as Aristotle suggests, some *single* final end of human life. It does seem to me possible that a person might seek to realize a plurality of ends without considering whether they are linked together under some more encompassing end.

Notes

1. The opening sentences of Aristotle, *Nicomachean Ethics: Translation, Introduction, and Commentary*, Sarah Broadie and Christopher Rowe (Oxford: Oxford University Press, 2002), bk. I, ch. 1, §1094a.
2. Ibid., bk. III, ch. iii, §1112b11–1113a2; cf. *Eudemian Ethics*, 1226b10–14, 1227a5–15, b23–33. Cf. also David Hume: "Reason is, and ought only to be the slave of the passions, and can never pretend to any other office than to serve and obey them. . . . 'Tis not contrary to reason to prefer the destruction of the whole world to the scratching of my finger," *A Treatise of Human Nature*, bk. II, ch. 3, §iii.
3. When it comes to explicating *eudaimonia*, Aristotle searches for something distinctive about humans that might constitute their "function"—their capacity for rational thought—and then goes on to characterize "the good of man [as] an activity of the soul in conformity with excellence or virtue, and if there are several virtues, in conformity with the best and most complete," *Nicomachean Ethics*, bk. 1, ch. 7, §1098a.
4. In speaking of action, I generally have *voluntary* human action in mind and not mere bodily movements, though most human action is expressed through conduct

involving bodily movements. (Further elaborations—there are many—belong elsewhere.)

5. There is the additional complication that "end" can be used in either a "task" or "outcome" sense—as something at which we aim, or state of affairs that we actually achieve. So *eudaimonia* may be said to be something that we seek to realize or that we achieve. Aristotle makes the distinction between "activities" and "products of activities," giving priority to the latter when they are produced. Because our interest here is in practical reasoning, we will for the most part focus on ends as reasons for action rather than on outcomes, recognizing that the realization of the outcome takes some kind of normative priority over the teleological activity. [Sometimes we may speak of an end or outcome that has not been aimed at. For example, the end (as outcome or result) of a stop-and-frisk by a NY police officer of a 14-year-old boy was discovery of a concealed handgun, though the legitimacy of the stop-and-frisk was dismissed by the Appellate Division of the State Supreme Court because the officer lacked adequate cause to search him. See *Matter of Darryl C*, 2012 NY Slip Op 05118 (June 26), available at: www.nycourts.gov/reporter/3dseries/2012/2012_05118.htm.]
6. For some influential discussions, see G.E. Moore, "The Concept of Intrinsic Value," in *Philosophical Studies* (London: Routledge & Kegan Paul, 1922), 253–75; Monroe C. Beardsley, "Intrinsic Value," *Philosophy & Phenomenological Research* 26 (1965–66): 1–17; Carl Wellman, *Morals & Ethics*, 2nd ed. (Englewood Cliffs, NJ: Prentice Hall, 1988), ch. 4. More generally, and for more recent discussions, see Michael Zimmerman, "Intrinsic v. Extrinsic Value," *The Stanford Encyclopedia of Philosophy*, 2010 ed., ed. Edward N. Zalta, available at: http://plato.stanford.edu/entries/value-intrinsic-extrinsic/.

   For the purposes of this study, I shall assume that what is deemed valuable is also valued, and that value is attributed to ends, means, or whatever by agents, though they generally employ certain criteria in deeming things to be valuable. In other words, I am sympathetic to the general thrust of Wittgenstein's remark: "The sense of the world must lie outside the world. In the world everything is as it is, and everything happens as it does happen: in it no value exists—and if it did exist, it would have no value," in *Tractatus Logico-Philosophicus*, trans. C.K. Ogden (1921), 6.41, available at: www.kfs.org/~jonathan/witt/tlph.html/.
7. As Ludwig Wittgenstein once put it in another context: "A picture held us captive. And we could not get outside it for it lay in our language and language seemed to repeat it to us inexorably," in *Philosophical Investigations*, trans. G.E.M. Anscombe (Oxford: Blackwell, 1953), §115.
8. See, e.g., John Dewey, *Human Nature and Conduct: An Introduction to Social Psychology* (New York: Modern Library, 1922).
9. See Abraham Edel, Irving Horowitz, and Peter Hare, *The Theory and Practice of Philosophy* (Piscataway, NJ: Transaction Books, 2008), 212ff.
10. I suspect that one of the reasons he thinks this is because the belief that there are objective ends will motivate some people to force others to conform to them—especially if they are seen as general ends of human life. But, as noted earlier, it could well be the case that such ends would be undermined were people forced to conform to them. Are people free if they are "forced to be free"?
11. Dewey discusses ends and means in many places, including *Human Nature and Conduct*, chap. 6; and "Theory of Valuation," in *International Encyclopedia of Unified Science*, ed. Otto Neurath (Chicago: University of Chicago Press, 1939), ch. 6.
12. Dewey, *Human Nature and Conduct*, 225, (*emphasis in original*).
13. "It is at least a sign of immaturity when an individual fails to view his end as also a moving condition of further consequences, thereby treating it as final in the sense

that 'final' signifies that the course of events has come to a complete stop," "Theory of Valuation," 44.

14. As we will soon see, however, that may even be true of final ends. Harry Frankfurt draws attention to the confusion (by G.E. Moore, among others) of ends in themselves with goods-in-themselves. What is chosen as an end in itself may not be chosen because it is good in itself. A final end may be chosen because of the various activities to which it gives rise as part of its pursuit and not just because of its inherent value. See "On the Usefulness of Final Ends," reprinted in Harry G. Frankfurt, *Necessity, Volition, and Love* (Cambridge: Cambridge University Press, 1999), 86–7. The paper originally appeared in *Iyyun*, 41 (1992): 3–19.
15. That which is an end to some means can become a means to a further end. Cf. Leon Trotsky: "in practical life . . . the end and the means constantly change places," in Leon Trotsky, John Dewey, and George Novack, *Their Morals and Ours: Marxist versus Liberal Views on Morality: Four Essays* (New York: Pathfinder Press, 1973), 19. Also: "A means can be justified only by its end. But the end in its turn needs to be justified. From the Marxist point of view, which expresses the historical interests of the proletariat, the end is justified if it leads to increasing the power of man over nature and to the abolition of the power of man over man. . . . That is permissible . . . which really leads to the liberation of mankind. Since this end can be achieved only through revolution, the liberating morality of the proletariat of necessity is endowed with revolutionary character" (40–41). (Trotsky's essay was published following the Moscow Trials of 1936–1938, in which he and others were convicted of capital crimes by the Stalinist government of Russia. We will later return to Trotsky's essay.)
16. For an elaboration, see Joel Feinberg, "Absurd Self-Fulfillment," in *Time and Cause*, ed. Peter van Inwagen (Dordrecht: D. Reidel, 1980): 255–81.
17. Frankfurt, *Necessity, Volition, and Love*, 87. Some writers make a distinction between "intrinsic" and "inherent" value. I am inclined to use them interchangeably, even though there may be some contexts in which one is to be preferred to the other.
18. We tackle that issue in Chapter 5.
19. Donald Hubin, "The Groundless Normativity of Instrumental Rationality," *Journal of Philosophy* 98 (2001): 467. See also David Gauthier, "Reason takes the ends of our activities as given, and determines the means to those ends," "Reason and Maximization," in *Moral Dealing: Contract, Ethics, and Reason* (Ithaca, NY: Cornell University Press, 1990), 211. Such a view is very common in domains that operate with economic cost-benefit models of rationality.
20. Christine Korsgaard, "The Normativity of Instrumental Reason," in *Ethics and Practical Reason*, ed. Garrett Cullity and Berys Nigel Gaut (Oxford: Oxford University Press, 1997), 220.
21. For more nuanced understandings of Aristotle (and Hume), see e.g.: Henry S. Richardson, *Practical Reasoning about Final Ends* (Cambridge, UK: Cambridge University Press, 1994). Also, Alfred R. Mele, "Aristotle and the Justification of Ends," *Proceedings of the Catholic Philosophical Association* 56 (1982): 79–86; Adrian M.S. Piper, "Hume on Rational Final Ends," *Philosophy Research Archives* 14 (1998–99): 193–228.
22. *Westminster Shorter Catechism*. http://www.westminsterconfession.org/confessional-standards/the-westminster-shorter-catechism.php.
23. In the present context, I make no distinction between "reasonable" and "rational." For an account that distinguishes them, see John Rawls, *A Theory of Justice* (Cambridge, MA: Harvard/Belknap, 1971), 419–20.
24. Augustine of Hippo, *Confessions*, bk. 1, ch. 1. Cf. Blaise Pascal, *Pensées* (New York: Penguin, 1966), 75: "What else does this craving, and this helplessness, proclaim

but that there was once in man a true happiness, of which all that now remains is the empty print and trace? This he tries in vain to fill with everything around him, seeking in things that are not there the help he cannot find in those that are, though none can help, since this infinite abyss can be filled only with an infinite and immutable object; in other words by God himself."

25. The characterization of certain ends as final in the sense that they might be invoked to justify the use of particular means need not be thought of as self-evident or unchallengeable. As we noted, part of Dewey's attack on such ends seems to be premised on the view that acceptance of such ends will lead to utopianism and fanaticism. What he sees as (acceptable) "ends-in-view"—that is, ends which, after a process of deliberation we have chosen to pursue—might reasonably be construed as final ends. Another reason for Dewey's attack on the notion of final ends reflects his interesting view that we do not arrive at ends-in-view without some consideration of the means that would be necessary to realize them. Means and ends, therefore, are not to be conceived of independently. Moreover, as Frankfurt points out, the value of a particular end may depend in part on the value it imparts to the means by which it is to be pursued. See "On the Usefulness of Final Ends," 90–1. Frankfurt's discussion, to which I merely allude here, indicates a much more complex dialectic of ends and means. Hence, the paradoxical title of his essay.

Chapter 2

The Ends of Policing

> Police are occupied by peacekeeping—but preoccupied with crime fighting.[1]

> Even though police perform an increasingly wide range of functions, it is crime control which remains uppermost in the perceptions of the police role in the minds of both the police and the public.[2]

Leaving to one side the plausibility of some grand general (ultimate) end of human action such as *eudaimonia*, it is now time to focus more narrowly on the ends of policing—a particular kind of human activity structured and constrained by certain limited (though not necessarily timeless) social ends.

It is fair to say that some policing function is as old as human society, insofar as there has always been a need to resolve human conflict and constrain human social behavior. As long as we have been acquainted with them, humans have not only been social creatures but also sometimes (oftentimes?) prone to getting in each other's way, necessitating some social mechanisms for dealing with this—in some cases judges, priests, kings, tribal elders, or wise men; in other cases institutions or other social control and enforcement mechanisms. It has rarely been thought sufficient to leave such resolutions to the unsupervised initiatives of individuals.

We might like to think that a community's "morality" should constitute the primary social mechanism for mediating human relations, and in a way, it is. We can view it as a set of relational understandings necessitated by human vulnerabilities and the tendency of humans to come into conflict. Thought of informally and individually, however, morality has been inadequate to the task. More formal mechanisms have been needed, and have included educational, religious, mediatorial, or governmental institutions, and, especially in liberal societies, the rule of law—mechanisms not always sharply differentiated. Recourse to these mechanisms of social control does not eschew moral concerns, but gives them voice in the public sphere. The more formal institutions to which we appeal must themselves be and usually are open to moral scrutiny.

As a definable formal institution in the modern sense, policing is a recent innovation, despite the presence of relatively formalized precursors in many ancient cultures—for example China, Israel, Greece, Rome, and, of course, England.[3]

The universal but diversely expressed need for a policing function may lead us to wonder whether there is something generally and universally referable to as "the ends of policing." At least in its institutionalized forms, policing has served a variety of ends, from securing citizens against violations by others to the maintenance of societal or class divisions to the protection of an existing regime against challenge by its subjects. Our concern here, though, will be with policing within the framework of a liberal democratic polity, in which societal constraints are answerable not only to popular will, but also to considerations of justice.[4] And that brings us to the modern era.

What—in most Western liberal democracies—we now think of as policing is ordinarily traced to the 1829 formation of the London Metropolitan Police Force, whose original handbook, authored by Charles Rowan and Richard Mayne, stated that "the principal object to be attained is '*the Prevention of Crime*'."[5] Beyond prevention, Rowan and Mayne perceived as a further end of policing "security of person and property [and] the preservation of public tranquility," both of which they believed to be "better effected" by the prevention (rather than the punishment) of crime.[6] The prevention of crime (along with the detection and prosecution of offenders) is not seen as a final end, but as means to securing certain other social values, and the success of a police force is to be determined by its ability to contribute to the latter. These other social values might be seen as final ends, albeit not the most final (ultimate) end. Security, though, and public tranquility, were seen as either elements of or as means to human flourishing (*eudaimonia*).

Before we look more carefully at this statement of the ends of policing, let me first relate it to some of the foregoing discussion about intermediate and final ends. Viewed socially, the value of policing is instrumental in that it serves the social purpose of preventing, detecting, and (more ultimately) punishing crime—social purposes that advance further purposes, those of social security and tranquility. That does not mean that policing cannot also be seen as a final, or even ultimate, end. Someone who becomes a police officer may identify with the social role to the point that serving in that role is seen as an end in itself or valuable for its own sake—indeed, as that which gives life its meaning. We may even *want* police officers to see their work in that way because the commitment it expresses is likely to manifest itself in more productive and competent work—especially given that the work in question can involve significant risk taking. Nevertheless, that which one values for its own sake may not always be valuable, or its value may be corrupted. And that which is valued for its own sake may not be the only thing to be valued for its own sake—thus raising the necessity for some prioritization. Moreover, we may wonder whether "the blue wall of silence" sometimes manifests commitment of officers to their role in a way that corrupts its larger social purpose.

Let me now get back to the substantive issue of policing's ends. The position taken in the London Metropolitan Police instructions (in their original or expanded form) reflects, or is at least consistent with, some much earlier theoretical statements about the ends of policing. Predating some earlier writings that anticipate the modern liberal democratic police force,[7] and already marking the distinction from French policing that the London Metropolitan Police was intended to represent,[8] one of the pioneers of liberal democratic thinking, John Locke, in his 1689 *Second Treatise Of Civil Government*, offered a rationale for policing being seen in much the way that it is viewed in the 1829 instructions.

In what might be seen as a digest of his position, Locke reflects on the importance of a civil order.[9] He begins with the idea that individual human beings possess certain fundamental rights—namely, the rights to "life, liberty, and property."[10] Locke speaks of these rights as the endowment of God (much as does the US Declaration of Independence, whose formulation was influenced by Locke), but secular versions of the idea are also implicit in the way he links the possession of rights to normative implications of the human capacity for rational and autonomous thinking.

However we construe fundamental rights, Locke argues that outside a civil order, the enjoyment of our rights is uncertain and likely to be imperiled. He does this by appealing to the theoretical notion of a "state of nature"—that is, a social order in which humans live in the absence of any formal rules or institutions of government. In that hypothesized pre-civil state (which Locke allows may involve *some* forms of communal life), benefit from the rights that people have will be haphazard, even though, because of their rational powers, individuals are capable of making judgments about how to conduct their lives.[11] Locke sees as the reason for this haphazardness both human limitations and ill will. Although Locke may well have constructed his argument against the theological background of his time (the frailty and perversity of human nature), his contention also resonates fairly well with our actual human experience.[12] Locke suggests that the broad failure of humans either to secure, or be secure in the exercise of, their rights leads (even flawed) rational beings such as we are to form social institutions that give us a better chance of exercising our rights. Security in our rights is for Locke, as it is for us, of critical importance.

Of course, living under rules of our own making involves some trade-offs: we vest some of our powers in the state and constrain some of our rights in order to ensure the more secure enjoyment of our remaining powers and rights. One thing we would relinquish—or at least limit—is our right of retaliation against those who violate our rights. This would now become the task of civil government to ensure. We would also give up some of our liberty insofar as we would place ourselves under a legal regime that would constrain our social life. Locke does not think of this as permanent alienation—what we do is "loan" our natural entitlements by authorizing others to act on our behalf. In the case of police, they remain part of the citizenry, but we empower them to do professionally what we are not capable of doing well as individuals acting independently. It is Locke's opinion, and he obviously sees it as reasonable, that we gain far more than we give up through this process.

Locke is explicit about the requisites and benefits of the civil order that needs to be established. He identifies three institutional mechanisms that characterize it. These make up for deficits in the state of nature. The first he identifies as the institution of law—a structure of social authority (a legislature) that determines the broad parameters of social conduct. Although Locke is committed to the idea that there is a natural moral order that is accessible to all, he believes that humans perceive and respond to it in different ways and cannot easily find or agree to solutions to their disputes. It is not that Locke wants to replace morality with law. Rather, his expectation is that the law will—for the most part—be consistent with morality and be open to change if there is moral criticism of it. Indeed, the institution of a legal order may be the best that morality can do regarding human social life (once the human community has reached a particular social mass and complexity).

There is, of course, nothing in Locke's proposal that ensures that the laws passed by a legislature will be acceptable to all. A legislature can be tyrannical and it can be misguided in what it prescribes and/or proscribes. However, for Locke, certain inbuilt constraints limit what a legislature may determine for a community. First of all, since the whole point of having such an institution is to secure, in the best way possible, the enjoyment of fundamental rights, a legislature that compromises those rights without a morally acceptable trade in security will exceed its justificatory bounds and lose its raison d'être. Second, Locke sees the formation of a legislature as something to which rational people will agree, and it is unlikely that they would agree to a serious compromise of their rights or to a compromise that was not accompanied by a greater enjoyment of the important—though constrained—rights that remained. We might reasonably accept constraints on the speed at which we drive motor vehicles as a reasonable trade for increased safety. If, however, what is up for trade is not simply our freedom to drive at the speed that we wish but what we often refer to as "civil liberties," then the bar is greatly raised. Civil liberties touch on the core of our fundamental rights, and their curtailment requires a much greater justification.[13]

Controversies about "reasonable constraints" mean that there is an ongoing debate about the limits of law—that is, the extent to which legislators may intrude on liberty—both generally with regard to the administration of daily life—laws dealing with commerce, property, contract, torts, and so on, and especially criminal law, which sanctions state punishment.

Beyond the establishment of a legislative process, Locke sees the necessity for a judiciary, an institution that judges matters of contention. It is one thing to have laws designed to ensure the maximal enjoyment of our fundamental rights. It is another to interpret and apply them. Locke is concerned that people are likely to interpret laws in ways that favor their own situation and are inclined to take too little interest in securing (legal) justice for others whose legal rights have been breached. So, we need a special institution that will have as its task both the interpretation of laws and their fair application. The institution of the judiciary will be constrained, ultimately, by the need to ensure the exercise of rights and to justify the broad grant of power over those to whom the laws are intended to apply. The judiciary may also function to constrain the activities of lawmakers and pass judgment on particular laws, determining whether or not they conform to the principles of their establishment. (This role is often seen as an aspect of the "checks and balances" that prevent one part of a governing civil order from gaining too much power relative to the other parts.)

Finally, Locke claims that because in a state of nature people who trespass on others are unlikely to voluntarily present themselves as violators and readily accept whatever judgment is made against them, the stronger will prevail against the weaker. So, we need institutional mechanisms to ensure that when instituted laws are broken, there is a mechanism in place for their enforcement. Thus, Locke sees a role for what we now characterize as policing as well as correctional institutions, and those who will fill the positions required by these roles.

We therefore find in Locke a rationale for the ends of policing that approaches the rationale outlined in the London Metropolitan Police Force *General Instructions*. I say "approaches" for two reasons. First, the Introduction to the Metropolitan Police *Instructions* puts its primary emphasis on prevention rather than on apprehension or on prosecution, for it recognizes that a society is likely to be better off if people are deterred from breaking the law rather than merely punished for it if they do. Not everyone who breaks the law will be caught and convicted. Indeed, it is often complained that policing is a poor deterrent since only a relatively small proportion of those who commit crimes are actually arrested for and convicted of them.[14] Moreover, the process of detecting, apprehending, and prosecuting suspects is likely to be more socially costly and disruptive than deterring them in the first place. The early *Instructions* envisaged a situation in which uniformed police officers would be sufficiently ubiquitous to dissuade those who might be tempted into criminality from acting upon such temptations.[15]

The second reason is that although the London Metropolitan Police *Instructions* focus specifically and almost exclusively on crime, presumably on deliberate or intentional violations of rights, Locke can be interpreted as holding that we should be discouraged not merely from deliberate violations of the law but also from negligence or administrative disorder, and so Locke probably envisions a far greater array of legislative initiatives and mechanisms for effecting them than the policing mandate indicates.

Do we wish to limit the ends of policing to those suggested by the Metropolitan Police focus—the prevention, detection, and prosecution of crime? We need not question the centrality of "law enforcement" or crime prevention, etc. to police work in order to suggest that it should be viewed more broadly. When the London Metropolitan Police Force was formed, there is no doubt that it was purposed largely in anti-crime terms. The blight of crime generated a need for some improved institutional response, and the Metropolitan Police joined with a number of other institutions that were already operating to make more effective and socially fairer inroads on crime.

Nevertheless, a closer review of the original *General Instructions* makes it clear that the police role was not viewed as narrowly as the initial statement seems to indicate. The vigilance of the constable also extended to public safety in a broad sense. Police were to be aware of a range of socially disruptive events such as fires and other safety hazards, and to take appropriate action with regard to them.

Once we begin to think of the institution of policing as an instance of governmental authority (as the London force was), we may find that with the evolution of our understanding of governmental authority, there will be a corresponding evolution in our understanding of the police role. The evolution of governmental authority is not something that occurs in vacuo, but in response to evolving social demands and, perhaps as well, changes in social self-perception. As we now encounter it, policing's "core concern with crime" constitutes less than half of what is expected of police.[16] No doubt we could argue that these other activities fall to police simply because they are "there," 24/7, even though they are not genuine constituents of the police role. But I think this overly narrows our contemporary understanding of the range of governmental services that we may expect and who may best be called upon to provide them. Many police departments reflect this understanding in denominating themselves departments of "public safety" (though I think that my social peacekeeping characterization offers a somewhat richer account).

* * *

I should make it clear that the foregoing discussion is intended to be normative—it is a discussion about what the role of police *should* be, and is intended to mesh reasonably well—at least in liberal democratic societies—with what policing *attempts to be*. There are writers who see a radical divide between popular conceptions of police work (as it *is* and *ought to be*) and how policing *actually functions* in society. For example, in their chapter on

"The Myth that the Role of Police is to Fight Crime," the Barlows point out that crimefighting constitutes a minor part of police work, but then use that claim—as a fair sociological statement—as part of a critique of policing in liberal democracies, viz.:

> the truth about policing is that throughout the history of our country [United States], it has served as a mechanism of social control designed to preserve the status quo in relations of power in society.[17]

This, of course, is not a recommendation for how police work ought to define itself, but an attempt to claim that we have been deceived as to the role of police work. And this is part of a larger critique of liberal democracies for being—or becoming—agencies of social control in which a smallish elite maintains its hegemony over others.

There is, no doubt, enough truth in this view about the role of policing—as there is in the view that policing is about crimefighting—to give it some plausibility, especially in a country such as the United States, which is still shadowed by its slave-owning and racist past (and present). But the response to the Barlows' claim, insofar as we see it to be true, is not to seek to shut down the police but (1) to work for a more egalitarian liberal democracy, and (2) to recast the police role in the light of that change. At a certain level, insofar as police serve the law as construed by the powers that be, they will almost always function in a socially conservative manner. The task is to ensure that the society and its laws that they serve are more egalitarianly structured.

* * *

Locke focused fairly exclusively on certain basic or fundamental rights—as he stated it, rights to life, liberty, and property—though it is clear that it is feeling and being secure in those rights that he also has in mind. For this reason, one might well want to argue that he recognized an underlying right to security that goes along with those to life, liberty, and property.

Locke's concern with what we have a right to raises a number of questions. First, one might question particular items on his list, namely, life, liberty, and property. The rights to life and liberty (though variously interpreted) are rarely challenged, but claims to a right to property have proven more problematic. For one thing, it is not clear just what constitutes "*private* property." Locke understands private property in more than one way. But more fundamentally, the validity of claims to a natural right to property may itself be questioned. Although the French Declaration of the Rights of Man and of Citizen explicitly refers to a fundamental right to property, the US Declaration of Independence speaks only of a right to the pursuit of happiness. The US Constitution does recognize property rights, but does not see those rights as fundamental, stating only that those who are deprived of their property must be justly compensated.

We might ask: In the exercise of which rights should the civil order be expected to secure us? How are we to interpret those rights? What role should the police have in ensuring these rights? (These are three large questions, and I shall offer here only the sketchiest of answers to them, answers intended to show only how deeply the subject of a police role is embedded in larger social and political issues.)

Let us turn from the limited listings of rights to be found in Locke's writings and also the Declaration of Independence to the long list of rights enumerated in the UN Universal Declaration of Rights (1948) or the catalogues of rights included in the later—and supposedly mandatory—UN Covenants. The UN documents have not gained universal acceptance and even within the domain of liberal democratic civil polities, there will be disagreement as to what governments should seek to secure for their citizens and how they should go about doing so. Contemporary debates among proponents of conservative, liberal, and libertarian perspectives on governmental obligations vis-à-vis citizens hint at the complexity here.

We should remember, though, that even agreement on what rights we have does not ensure agreement on the *interpretation* of those that are agreed upon. For example, some have argued that Locke's fundamental rights are to be interpreted negatively, so that the right to life is to be understood only as a right not to be killed, and the right to liberty is to be understood only as a right to non-interference. But some later writers have interpreted the rights not only positively, but also as including the wherewithal for their enjoyment. According to those writers, the right to life includes the provisions needed to *sustain* life (subsistence rights), and the right to liberty is understood as a right to effective choice (welfare rights). D.G. Ritchie, in a famous riposte to Herbert Spencer, who viewed rights negatively, argued that:

> In this country no one is hindered by law from reading all the works of Mr. Herbert Spencer. This is negative liberty. But if a man cannot read at all, or if he can read but has not any money to spare for the purpose of buying so many volumes, or if he has no access to any public library, or if the managers of any library to which he has access refuse to permit such works on their shelves, or, if having access to them, he has no leisure in which to read them, or if he has not had such an education as to enable him to understand what he reads, he cannot be said to get much good out of the fact that the law of the land does not prohibit him from reading Mr. Spencer's works.[18]

The debates over what specific fundamental rights we have, and how they are to be understood, continue to this day. They are broadly reflected in the left/right political divisions that remain active within liberal democracies.

I do not wish to diminish the importance of "crimefighting" to policing. Its centrality is shown, at least in many liberal democracies, by the powers that we give police to do their work—power to arrest and power over life and death. But these powers are among many that we vest in them. They are also charged with crowd management, the maintenance of public order, and expected to operate as crisis managers. Indeed, only a fraction of police officers' time is spent in crimefighting. For this reason, I am inclined to characterize the end of modern policing more broadly as one of social peacekeeping. Insofar as crime upsets the good ordering of our social lives, then crimefighting is an aspect of social peacekeeping.

This characterization of police work has at least three salient merits.[19]

1. It displays an historical link with an old tradition of policing and thus resonates with a conception of policing as securing the "King's Peace"—a zone of tranquility that the King's presence was intended to ensure. (It was seen as a duty of the Crown to provide for the protection of subjects, and though this was separate from the regular laws, it touches centrally on the security that is critical to social contract theory.)[20]

In a criticism of this historical allusion, Jeffrey Reiman complains that:

> linking a modern-day conception of the police as peacekeepers to the notion of the "king's peace" does little more than exploit a verbal similarity. It is not even clear that the king's peace should be thought of as historically continuous with present-day police forces, since the king's peace was a late-feudal development and today's police are a response to modern industrialization (large and mobile urban proletariats and so on). The king's peace was enforced by magistrates and sheriffs; it predates modern policing by hundreds of years.[21]

Reiman is right about the important differences between the King's Peace, as originally construed, and the notion of social peacekeeping that I advance. The early King's Peace was the concomitant of a special royal prerogative rather than an intended outcome of the extant law. Nevertheless, in the British Commonwealth, the (current) Queen's Peace still exists as a social order that the monarch is bound to provide for her subjects, and is reflected in the terminology for disturbing the social order: "breaching the peace."[22] We might compare this historical resonance with the resonance that modern human rights regimes, such as the European Convention on Human Rights (1950+), have with the Magna Carta, a feudal document (1215). Even now, we rarely discuss the development of human rights without some reference to the Magna Carta, even though what is enshrined in that document differs significantly from what we now see as liberal democratic rights. The distance that Reiman sees between the King's Peace and today's social peacekeeping is not as dramatic or discontinuous as he makes out. On the contrary, insofar as the focus of the King's Peace was the sovereign's commitment to the safety of subjects, I think the connections are quite substantive. Modern divisions of human labor reach deeply into our human past, and although the form that such labor takes is dependent on socio-historical circumstances, the interests to which it responds are grounded in common and trans-national human experience.

Reiman further argues that:

> the keepers of the king's peace did not engage in dispute resolution or emergency medical service. What they did was closer to the law enforcement, crime-fighting function that Kleinig wants to expand beyond—and that is the sympathetic interpretation of the king's peace. The critical interpretation is that the work of the keepers of the king's peace was that of wresting criminal justice out of the hands of local communities and establishing on the ground the monopoly on coercion that defines the nation state in theory.[23]

To respond: it is *not* my view that there is some identity of understanding or purpose between those who kept the King's Peace and modern day policing.[24] It is also not clear to me on what basis[25] Reiman claims that keepers of the King's peace sought to *remove* criminal justice from local communities and relocate it as a non-negotiable power with the king. Those who became keepers of the peace were assigned to unruly parts of the realm to enforce existing law, not to take over a working system and change it.[26]

2. The second merit of my view that policing is a form of social peacekeeping is that social peacekeeping captures a range of police functions that do not have a lot to do with law enforcement—the maintenance of public order through crowd and traffic control, and responsiveness to various social emergencies, only some of which involve crime. My view does not diminish or belittle the crimefighting role of police, but embeds it in a larger social task to which police are called.[27]

Reiman takes issue with my view, as stated earlier, arguing the fact that "police are armed (and dressed in military-style uniforms) for law enforcement" dictates the way in which they engage in "crowd and traffic control. . . . [i]f a small group of individuals is to keep a large, unpredictable and potentially dangerous group in line, it will certainly help if the small group is armed and in distinctive dress." So, "[r]ather than alternatives to the crimefighter role, it seems that crowd and traffic control are direct extensions of that role."[28]

Once again, I think that Reiman is only partly correct. Apart from the fact that he reflects what might be taken to be an American experience of policing (in which police are always armed), there are real dangers if, in their crowd and traffic control roles, police emphasize their coercive power (rather than have it as a resource if and when needed). We have seen this in the case of public protests, which are often handled more judiciously through prior negotiation and a hands-off approach than one that confrontationally emphasizes the power that is available to them. Current controversies about the militarization of police and the overuse of SWAT teams reflect just the kind of connection that Reiman emphasizes. But Reiman's characterization of the police role is, as I argue, a degradation of the police role rather than its natural development.[29]

There is no doubt that development of the police role—assuming that it began as something as narrow as crimefighting, took the course it did, as do all social occupations, in response to pressing social demands. It's certainly true of academics and mayors. With social evolution, things that once did not "fall" to police, academics, and mayors now do, and some things that once "fell" to them have become the responsibility of others. As first and 24/7 responders to social crises, criminal and non-criminal, police are likely to find themselves called upon to perform tasks that are not at all crime-related. Indeed, they now receive training for such tasks—whether delivering babies, administering naloxone, or providing CPR. And, if individual first-line police officers do not receive training to deal with special needs, specialist police units are often created for this purpose—juveniles, the mentally disturbed, and so forth. Reiman loses sight of the fact that only a minor (albeit very important) portion of police work is now focused on crimefighting activities, and much the larger portion of their job is focused on peacekeeping activities.[30] This goes hand in hand with changing conceptions of what we may reasonably expect a government to provide. Reiman sees crowd and traffic control as socially intelligible extensions to crime control—I suggest that keeping the social peace is the rationale for extending police to crowd and traffic control.

Furthermore, I believe Reiman is incorrect to see the police uniform as military-style.[31] Certainly the role and uniform of a London Bobby was intended to be differentiated from that of a soldier. The uniform symbolizes a certain kind of standardized authority that extends beyond the individual to the role. No doubt there have been times—such as our own—when police authority has sometimes trended in a military direction,[32] but such militarization has been an occasion for vigorous criticism rather than treated as normal or acceptable.[33] Moreover, although Americans have acclimatized themselves to seeing their police armed, this has happened in other places, largely as changing social circumstances have made the role of police more dangerous.

Reiman's objection to the characterization of police as social peacekeepers has a deeper point, connected to his broader social analysis of policing. As he puts it, the emergency medical and social assistance that police offer is "not normally performed by the police for society as a whole. They are largely performed for the poor." He contends that middle class and wealthier people "do not turn to the police for dispute resolution or assistance in medical emergencies." Instead, they go to experts—lawyers, psychiatrists, and doctors. That police perform certain welfare roles is, he claims, "due to the larger society's failure to provide for the poor the specialized services that are available for a price to the better off."[34]

I do not wish to deny some aspects of the larger social critique that Reiman has in mind, or that the poor are more likely to make greater use of police services than others. The social peacekeeping role that police have acquired should not serve as a substitute for the availability of these services from other sources, whether publicly funded or not. Insofar as police accept some of these social welfare roles, they do so as emergency operators and not as publicly funded providers. When police respond to emergencies, they do so without regard to whether those in need are rich or poor, even though they may be called to do less where those they respond to can afford more professionalized care.

Still, I am not certain what evidence Reiman has for claiming that police peacekeeping tasks such as dispute resolution and medical emergencies are "largely performed for the poor" or that they have been dumped on the police by a "powerful few," as he puts it.[35] Even if Reiman's claim is true, that would not undermine the social peacekeeping role of the police.

Reiman may be correct to see the "we" of social decision-making as reflecting less than "one mind" and a "single voice," but that might well be true of any social allocation. What may be of more importance to determine, is whether, in having police engage in dispute resolution and the dispensing of emergency medical assistance, they are being asked to engage in activities that might not be universally appreciated when provided. And I do not see that. Moreover, at least within liberal democratic communities, police do not usually comprise an oppressed minority with little power, and what they do and don't take on is as much within *their* power to determine or affect as that of others who have effective standing within the community.[36]

3. The third merit to seeing the ends of policing more broadly than crime control is that it deflects some attention from the use of force to which—because of the focus on crime control—many accounts of policing make explicit reference.[37] There is no doubt that the use of force is something that, socially, we largely confine to police (though exigencies may also support the formation and readiness of something like a national guard). Vesting most coercive social force in police is one of the sacrifices we make as a result of the (hypothetical) social contract. Not that all use of force is ceded, but where it is needed and police are available to use it, we generally consider it *their* prerogative to exercise it.[38] Nevertheless, the use of force, even in the case of police, is something that we grant as a second or last resort rather than a first one.[39] In the UK, the authority to arrest, and its implementation, may not involve any use of force (even if there is a symbolic "touching"). An arresting police officer may not be armed, and the requirement of compliance

need not even be accompanied by handcuffing. The power to arrest is to be thought of primarily as an acknowledged authority to which coercive force is secondary.

Reiman shows a degree of skepticism about deflection. He asserts that because both police and community take it for granted that police are basically "law enforcers," it is unlikely that there will be benefits to viewing them as social peacekeepers. He considers that one of the potential benefits—a reduced reliance on deadly force—has occurred in recent years "as a result of public outcry and legal decisions" without requiring any shift of paradigm from law enforcement to social peacekeeping.

Certainly, there has been some resistance (at least on the part of some police) to community policing, a form of policing that focuses as much on social cooperation as on enforcement. The reassertion of community policing (more easily assimilated to a social peacekeeping model) by police reformers and the more general public in the wake of "brutality" cases suggests to me that there is a greater willingness to see police as more than law enforcers. Moreover, the decreased use of deadly force has had some partial explanation in factors that are independent of broader perceptions of police work.[40] Deadly force is something of an outlier when compared to other uses of force, and the need for more de-escalation training in the handling of public disorder is where the focus should be. Such training views the use of coercive force as a later—rather than as a first—resort.

I have already suggested that law enforcement and social peacekeeping are not alternative characterizations of police work. Social peacekeeping incorporates law enforcement as one of its expressions—an important one, because police are the major repositories of intra-societal force. Law enforcement is unquestionably a police job. Reiman argues that advocating a social peacekeeping role for police is not likely to be accepted because it runs up against the deeply ingrained view of police as law enforcers. But this may show only that we have reaped its consequences, as we attempt to come to grips with the overuse of force—the use of tear gas or tasers when negotiation would have been preferable, the use of threat when a more nuanced use of authority would have been sufficient, and the unnecessary use or the misuse (say, by overtightening) of handcuffs. Were a different paradigm in place, social order maintenance might well be made easier.

Reiman has more to add: "the most salient fact about the police, the very thing that calls for special justification and for special accountability [is] that the police have the authority to order us around and to use violence to back those orders up." In Reiman's view, my claim that policing is basically about social peacekeeping overlooks "the specialness of the authority of the police to use force."[41]

There is no denying that the authority of police to use coercive force *is* special (and also in need of special justification). But so are some of the other authorities that police possess. Police are socially permitted to use deception and to infringe on privacy as part of their peacekeeping role, and though we may view the use of force as the most ethically problematic challenge that confronts them, we need to be careful that it does not so dominate our perception of what police do that we ignore or fail to attend to the other significant ethical challenges that confront them, such as those relating to truthfulness, privacy, and use of discretion. Underlying Reiman's position is an empirical claim; namely, that the social peacekeeping appellation obscures the specialness of police authority (to use force). I'm not convinced of that, and I'm not convinced by his contrast between the doctor and police officer. True, one may ignore a doctor in a way that one may not ignore a police officer. That, however, has more to do with the role that each has. I may no more ignore my boss than I may ignore a police officer—if I do, I may be fired, even if I may not be manhandled.

As it is, police have only a constrained authority to stop and question people. Even if people cannot ignore police officers' orders to stop or move, they do not have to speak with the officers (with the possible exception of providing their names; if arrested, they can assert their right to remain silent), under most circumstances people may refuse to be searched,[42] and may leave once they have ascertained that they are not under arrest. That, at least, is the law. Whether a particular police officer takes notice of it is, of course, another matter. My contention is that police authority is to be thought of as grounded primarily in a competence to maintain social peace, and although that authority may sometimes need to be backed up by force, it often accomplishes its purposes as a consequence of the competence associated with it.

Conclusion

Although the police do not have a timelessly fixed social role, one of the persisting and central elements of that role is the maintenance of order and the enforcement of law. It is this aspect of their role that justifies some of the special powers they have (such as the use of force, deception, and the infringement of privacy), in some cases as the more or less exclusive possessors of such powers. That is sometimes asserted to delimit their role, but this is too narrow a conception. It does not reflect the range of tasks that we expect police to perform; nor does it reflect the way in which police are actually deployed. I have suggested that if we are looking for some larger umbrella under which police work can be gathered, we do better to see their role as one of social peacekeeping. To see this as their primary role diverts us from overly focusing on one of their means—the use of force, including the use of lethal force (which should be used only in narrowly circumscribed circumstances). Police authority, and the competence that such authority is intended to express, is a recognition that, with respect to a range of actually and potentially disruptive social events, police are especially well-prepared to deal with them.

Notes

1. Jesse Rubin, "Police Identity and the Police Role," in *The Police and the Community*, ed. Robert F. Steadman (Baltimore: Johns Hopkins University Press, 1972), 25.
2. "Role of the Police," John Howard Society of Alberta, 1997, 5, available at: www.johnhoward.ab.ca/pub/C52.htm.
3. See, for example, Stephen M. Passamaneck, *Police Ethics and the Jewish Tradition* (Charles C. Thomas, 2003); Captain W.L. Melville Lee, *A History of Police in England* (London: Methuen, 1901), available at: http://archive.org/details/historyofpolicei00leewuoft; Markus Dirk Dubber, *The Police Power: Patriarchy and the Foundations of American Government* (New York: Columbia University Press, 2005). For a brief overview, see Philip Rawlings, *Policing: A Short History* (Cullompton, Devon: Willan, 2001); see, generally, Wikipedia Editors, "Police," available at: http://en.wikipedia.org/wiki/Police.
4. Even that, of course, presumes some agreement about justice generally, the justice of institutions, and the justice of societal norms. We should not presume that laws and the administration of justice in a liberal democratic society are "okay as given."
5. Metropolitan Police, *Instructions to Police Officers* (London: HMSO, 1829), 1 (*emphasis in original*). Oversight of the first Metropolitan Police was put in the hands of Lieutenant-Colonel Charles Rowan and Richard Mayne (a lawyer). Police detective work came a bit later (1842), that role initially being continued by Henry Fielding's Bow Street Runners (formed in 1744).
6. Metropolitan Police, *Instructions*, 1–2.
7. For example, Patrick Colquhoun, *A Treatise on the Police of the Metropolis* (London: C. Dilly, 1796), available at: www.gutenberg.org/ebooks/35650.
8. See Philip John Stead, *The Police of France* (London: Macmillan, 1983); Philip John Stead, *The Police of Britain* (London: Macmillan, 1985).
9. John Locke, *Second Treatise of Civil Government* (1689), ch. 9, available at: www.constitution.org/jl/2ndtreat.htm.
10. Later, when we look at the Kantian idea of persons as ends (Chapter 7), we will see some connections between the view that persons should be treated as ends and never as mere means and their individual possession of certain fundamental rights, including rights of autonomy.
11. That is, they are able to do what Locke refers to as "discern the law of nature."
12. There are, of course, traditions that argue for the essential rationality, goodness, and cooperativeness of humans, and which attribute what we see of human irrationality and ill will to the existence of corrupting social and economic structures, be they capitalist or communist. Though theoretically possible, and endorsed by many, this position is less credible than its followers suggest. "Humans as we find them" are notoriously limited, morally as well as rationally. For a psychological reflection on this, consider the work of the Nobel laureate Daniel Kahneman, *Thinking Fast and Thinking Slow* (New York: Farrar, Straus and Giroux, 2011).
13. There may, of course, be some dispute about what constitute our civil liberties—think for example about same-sex marriage or governmental eavesdropping. In some liberal democratic states, core liberties are enumerated in and secured by a constitution. Cf. the US Bill of Rights, or a more modern document such as the European Convention on Human Rights.
14. See, in general for the US, the FBI Uniform Crime Reports, noting clearance rates—e.g., www.fbi.gov/about-us/cjis/ucr/crime-in-the-u.s/2010/crime-in-the-u.s.-2010/

clearances-figure. Serious crimes do better than less serious ones, though far more less serious ones are committed.

15. Of course, deterrence may have its own costs. For example, the growing ubiquity of CCTV cameras and other monitoring devices might succeed in deterring crime, but with significant costs to privacy. And especially onerous punishments designed to act as general deterrents threaten serious injustice to some. See Michael Wines, "Illegal Voting Gets Texas Woman 8 Years in Prison, and Certain Deportation," *New York Times*, 2/10/2017, available at: www.nytimes.com/2017/02/10/us/illegal-voting-gets-texas-woman-8-years-in-prison-and-certain-deportation.html.
16. Much less than half, some would argue. See, especially, David H. Bayley, *Police for the Future* (New York: Oxford University Press, 1994).
17. David E. Barlow and Melissa Hickman Barlow, "The Myth That the Role of Police Is to Fight Crime," in *Demystifying Crime and Criminal Justice*, ed. Robert M. Bohm and Jeffrey T. Walker (Los Angeles: Roxbury, 2006), 74.
18. D.G. Ritchie, *Natural Rights* (London: Allen & Unwin, 1894), 139. On the so-called negative/positive debate, see W.L. Weinstein, "The Concept of Liberty in Nineteenth Century English Political Thought," *Political Studies* 13, no. 2 (1965): 145–63; Gerald C. MacCallum, Jr., "Negative and Positive Freedom," *The Philosophical Review* 76, no. 3 (1967): 312–34: and, more generally, Henry Shue, *Basic Rights: Subsistence, Affluence, and U.S. Foreign Policy*, 2nd ed. (Princeton, NJ: Princeton University Press, 1996), ch. 2.
19. See John Kleinig, *The Ethics of Policing* (Cambridge: Cambridge University Press, 1996), ch. 1.
20. I have focused more on the security aspect in John Kleinig, "Security and Police Ethics," in *Routledge Handbook on Ethics and Public Policy*, ed. Annabelle Lever and Andrei Poama (Abingdon, UK: Routledge, 2019), 91–101.
21. Jeffrey Reiman, Review Essay: "The Scope and Limits of Police Ethics," *Criminal Justice Ethics* 16, no. 2 (1997): 44.
22. The language of breaching the peace is preserved in the US Constitution, art 1.
23. Reiman, "The Scope and Limits of Police Ethics," 44.
24. Ironically, what Reiman acknowledges in making the distinction between then and now is central to my desire not to see contemporary policing as crimefighting or law enforcement but as social peacekeeping, where peacekeeping is a broad enough category to include crimefighting along with the other tasks he mentions—dispute resolution and the provision of emergency medical service.
25. Apart from Reiman's ideological framework—his generally Marxist critique of contemporary liberal democracies. See, for example, the many editions of his *The Rich Get Richer and the Poor Get Prison: Ideology, Crime and Criminal Justice* (Boston: Allyn & Bacon, from 1979 to the present).
26. See Charles Austin Beard, *The Office of Justice of the Peace in England, in Its Origin and Development* (New York: Burt Franklin, 1904).
27. In an influential statement of the police role, Herman Goldstein, catalogued the police functions as follows:

    - To prevent and control conduct widely recognized as threatening to life and property
    - To aid individuals who are in danger of physical harm, such as the victims of violent attack
    - To facilitate the movement of people and vehicles
    - To assist those who cannot care for themselves, the intoxicated, the addicted, the mentally ill, the physically disabled, the old, and the young
    - To resolve conflict, whether it be between individuals, groups or individuals, or individuals and their government

- To identify problems that have the potential for becoming more serious problems
- To create and maintain a feeling of security in communities

Policing a Free Society (New York: Ballinger, 1977), 35.

See also, American Bar Association, *Standards Relating to the Urban Police Function*, 1–2.2, available at: www.americanbar.org/publications/criminal_justice_section_archive/crimjust_standards_urbanpolice.html.

28. Reiman, "The Scope and Limits of Police Ethics," 44.
29. I have written about militarization in "What's All the Fuss about Police Militarization?," *The Critique*, March 17, 2015, available at: www.thecritique.com/articles/whats-all-the-fuss-with-police-militarization/. See, further, Ryan Welch and Jack Mewhirter, "Does Military Equipment Lead Police Officers to be More Violent? We Did the Research," *Washington Post*, 6/30/2017, available at: www.washingtonpost.com/news/monkey-cage/wp/2017/06/30/does-military-equipment-lead-police-officers-to-be-more-violent-we-did-the-research/?utm_term=.dcd7530e061f. On the perils of confrontational approaches, see P.A.J. Waddington, "Riot Control, Minimum Force, and the British Police Tradition," in *Policing, Organised Crime and Crime Prevention*, ed. R. Morgan (Bristol: Bristol and Bath Centre for Criminal Justice, 1991), 49–74.
30. It might be useful to reflect on the way in which, for most academics, their work has shifted from research to teaching (and administration).
31. No more so than the uniform of a doorman—though I accept that police uniforms (and rituals) have sometimes tended in that direction.
32. See John Paul and Michael L. Birzer, "Images of Power: An Analysis of the Militarization of Police Uniforms and Messages of Service," *Free Inquiry in Creative Sociology* 32, no. 2 (2004): 121–8.
33. See, for example, Peter B. Kraska (ed.), *Militarizing the American Criminal Justice System: The Changing Roles of the Armed Forces and the Police* (Boston, MA: Northeastern University Press, 2001).
34. Reiman, "The Scope and Limits of Police Ethics," 44–5.
35. The best I can suggest is that "middle class and richer folks" (Reiman, "The Scope and Limits of Police Ethics," 44) generally engage in their disputes or require assistance behind closed doors, out of the public eye, and that those with fewer means are likely to manifest their need for assistance more publicly. That would match a partial explanation of the fact that middle class whites are less likely to be apprehended for drug use than lower class blacks, despite comparable drug use.
36. In some US jurisdictions, police have resisted political pressures to surveil for illegal immigrants or even terrorist activity, believing that these activities should fall to other agencies. In other jurisdictions, often mirroring the local political ethos, they have readily engaged in such tasks.
37. In an influential account of policing, Egon Bittner wrote: "the role of police is to address all sorts of human problems when and insofar as the problems' solutions may require the use of force at the point of their occurrence," "The Capacity to Use Force as the Core of the Police Role," in *Moral Issues in Police Work*, ed. Frederick A. Elliston and Michael Feldberg (Totowa, NJ: Rowman & Allanheld, 1985), 21. Though Bittner claims only that the problems dealt with by police "*may* require the use of force" rather than that they need to do so, in the United States, arrest decisions that *may* have become a *must* (*emphasis added*).
38. Not, of course, that they may use it without accountability. Police authority is viewed as a grant rather than an independent possession.
39. In the United States, it is easy to lose sight of this, for there, as a matter of course, police are visibly armed and routinely handcuff those they arrest.

40. Lawrence Sherman, "Reducing Police Gun Use: Critical Events, Administrative Policy, and Organizational Change," in *Control in the Police Organization*, ed. Maurice Punch (Cambridge, MA: MIT Press, 1983), 98–125.
41. Reiman, "The Scope and Limits of Police Ethics," 45.
42. Much of the current debate about police stop-and-frisk practices concerns overreaching in this regard.

Chapter 3

Means

> They say, "means are, after all, means." I would say, "means are, after all, everything." As the means so the end. . . . There is no wall of separation between the means and the end.[1]

As the language of ends is sometimes replaceable by other terms, so too the language of means sometimes takes the form of a way, method, or instrument for bringing about some end or achieving some goal or purpose.[2]

What is meant by a *means* to an end can be ambiguous. On one account, what is characterized as a means to an end is construed simply as that which *enables* or *assists* in realizing an end. In this view, trees can be said to be one of the means whereby emitted CO_2 is removed from the atmosphere. A lever is used to move a heavy object. Mounted police provide an effective means of crowd control. The language in all of these cases is the language of causation: *A*'s use enables or assists in the bringing about of *B*. Where the means are intended by some agent to bring about some result, the language may be only that of an intended rather than an actual cause. So, *A* is a means to *B* may be understood to mean that *A* is intended to bring about *B*—whether or not *B* is actually brought about as a consequence of using *A*. For example, despite the use of mounted police, a riot may erupt.[3]

The range of things that can be characterized as means is very broad. Means may be objects, events, states of affairs, or actions. So far as the subject of this study is concerned, in which ends are often invoked to justify particular means, the means in question will usually comprise actions, albeit actions that will often employ objects, events, etc. as their intentional means. Police will thus conduct a sting operation as a means to counter rampant insurance fraud.

Often, the language of means is intended to suggest some *instrumental value*. That is, characterizing *A* as a means to *B* is to characterize *A* as instrumentally valuable for the purpose of realizing *B*. The assumption in such cases is that *B* is considered valuable (either in itself or as a means to some other end that is considered valuable in itself, or that it is desired for its own sake). Sometimes, if *A* is said to be an instrumentally valuable means to *B*, there may be a tacit assumption that *A* has no value apart from its relation to B—that, in itself, *A* is normatively or ethically neutral.[4] That is, it is assumed that any value *A* has is derived solely from the end that it serves.

Aristotle sometimes appears to presume that the value of means rests only upon the value of the ends they serve. This view is highly contentious and probably incorrect. One can easily see this by observing that a simple means-ends relation is often part of a much longer chain: *A* is a means to *B*, which may be a means to *C*, which, in turn, is a means to *D*, which, in turn, is a means to *E*, which is a means to *F* . . . and so on. What is thus seen as a means under one description is to be seen as an end under another description. Of course, the fact that *C* may be described as both means and end does not settle the question of the normative status of a particular means, because ends can sometimes be characterized descriptively. Nevertheless, to the extent that we wish to use ends to justify means, that which functions as both a means and an end will often be normatively characterizable apart from its value as a means.[5] Here I also suggest, in advance of a deeper exploration later, that where the means to ends are *actions*, they are evaluable not only in relation to the ends they lead to, but also by reference to their other—intrinsic and extrinsic—features.

The inadequacy of simply drawing a contrast between an end valued for its own sake and a means valued only because of the end it serves can also be seen when there might be more than one means. If Albert wants to get to from the West Side of Manhattan to the Upper East Side, he has a number of options open to him. He can walk, take a taxi, catch the subway, or go by bus. One of those might be the most efficient. But if efficiency is not particularly at issue, Albert may decide to get exercise by walking or to enjoy the sights of Manhattan via a bus trip. If the day is wet, Albert may decide that a taxi is his best option, even though it will cost more. Or, if the weather is too bad, and finding a taxi is not certain, he may decide to abandon going to the East Side altogether. We can see from this that the issue is not simply one of achieving the end, but of realizing it appropriately.

There may be no single, simple characterization of the view that the end gives value to means. It may be taken to claim that by virtue of the ends that they serve, means gain an evaluative significance. Or it may mean that, apart from their use to accomplish certain ends, means are evaluatively neutral. That is, the value *of* a means is its value *as* a means. Or, of course, it may mean both. Or there can be a different hybrid understanding: even if the means are not evaluatively neutral, some of their value may come from the ends that they serve.

The view that it is the ends that give the means, whatever value they have, has been given brutal expression in political thought. The controversial and oft-heard claim that one person's terrorist is another person's freedom fighter captures the point well enough[6]: it suggests that only the ends served by an act, regardless of how violent that act, are what give them their normative significance. Given different ends, with different normative assessments of those ends, particular means will be seen as either justified or unjustified. In the events surrounding the 1917 Russian Revolution, the view appears to have gained considerable support. A Cheka document states that "murder, lies and treachery are immoral and shameful if they are harmful to the proletarian revolution; these same lies, treachery and murder are moral and laudable if they serve this revolution."[7] The point is clear enough: what would be deemed murder, lies, and treachery, were they to harm the proletarian revolution, do not carry their usual negative normative weight when used to advance the (liberating) revolution.

That debate has a particular resonance in the controversy over Leon Trotsky's essay, "Their Morals and Ours," first published in 1938 in the *New International*.[8] Some background will help. Although Trotsky was unabashed in his support for the Communist Revolution, and in its early days was at its forefront, he was always a somewhat idiosyncratic and critical thinker and when Josef Stalin came to power he was increasingly marginalized and finally dismissed from the Party in 1927. He continued to criticize Stalin, however, and had to decamp to Norway. Matters came to a head in 1936–1938 when, at Stalin's behest, trials were staged in Moscow in which Trotsky, along with others, was accused and convicted of plotting against the Stalinist regime. Although he was no longer in Russia, the verdict led to his expulsion from Norway and subsequent resettlement in Mexico City, where he wrote "Their Morals and Ours."[9] At the time of the trials, John Dewey, who from 1904–1930 had been an influential professor of philosophy at Columbia University, and had written extensively on the means-end relation, chaired a commission to look into the trials' legitimacy and, as part of its work, he traveled to Mexico to interview Trotsky. He concluded that they were political purges rather than genuine trials, and when asked to respond to Trotsky's essay, he did so and, several months after Trotsky's was published, his response followed, also in the *New International*.

Trotsky's essay was intended as a refutation of Stalinist accusations. In it, one of his major purposes was to defend his own form of revolutionary socialism against the claim—with which he charges Stalinism—that revolutionary socialism adheres to the "amoralistic 'Jesuitical maxim'"—the end justifies the means—and thus stands in need of moral absolutes that will constrain means, no matter how valuable the end. Trotsky claims that those who argue for constraining absolutes speak from a position of "class" dominance and use those constraints as a way of containing threats to their dominant position. He writes that "the norms of 'obligatory' morality are filled with class, that is, antagonistic content."[10] Furthermore, when those who advocate such moral absolutes are themselves seriously challenged, they too abandon such constraints lest their ends be subverted.

Before we move further into Trotsky's argument, we might note two points. First, Trotsky's reference to the "Jesuitical" maxim may suggest that it had wide currency in Jesuit circles, a position that the Catholic Church explicitly denies.[11] Second, Trotsky himself, albeit no friend of the Jesuits, concedes that even those Jesuits who appeared to uphold the view that the end justifies the means "never taught . . . that any means, even though it be criminal from the point of view of the Catholic morals, was permissible if only it led to the 'end,' that is, to the triumph of Catholicism."[12] Rather, what they taught is that "the means in itself can be a matter of indifference but that the moral justification or condemnation of the given means flows from the end."[13] In other words, Trotsky argued that what the Jesuits taught was not that (important enough) ends make seriously immoral actions permissible, but that what gives means their value are the ends that they serve. As he puts it, the means do not carry their "own moral tag like merchandise with fixed prices in a department store."[14] Moreover, "in practical life . . . the end and the means constantly change places."[15] That which is an end to some means becomes itself a means to a further end.

Whether Trotsky or the Catholic Church were correct in their assertions is, perhaps, a matter of ongoing contention. However, in the epigraph to "The Second Hearing" in Arthur Koestler's *Darkness at Noon*, the pre-Jesuit Catholic historian, Dietrich von Nieheim, is supposedly quoted as saying:

> When the Existence of the Church is threatened, she is released from the commandments of morality. With unity as the end, the use of every means is sanctified, even cunning, treachery, violence, simony, prison, death. For all order is for the sake of the community, and the individual must be sacrificed to the common good.[16]

Perhaps the implication of that is not that means are morally neutral, but that the importance ascribable to the ends overrides any intrinsic disvalue that the means may have and thus justifies as means even "cunning, treachery, violence, simony, prison, death." One can see how, in contexts in which "the group" (of whatever kind) is made morally primary (or important enough), individuals may be sacrificed.[17]

Trotsky seeks to detail his defense of the view that his and Stalin's ends were different[18]: Whereas the Bolshevik revolution was a progressive movement designed to abolish privilege, wage war on social inequality, replace the bureaucracy with self-government of the toilers, and abolish secret diplomacy, and strove to render all social relationships completely transparent,[19] Stalinism was an "immense bureaucratic reaction against the proletarian dictatorship in a backward and isolated country."[20]

In Trotsky's view, what distinguishes *their* morals and *ours*—where *they* are represented on one hand by Stalinists and on the other by the bourgeoisie—is not some "abstract principle" (as he puts it) that places a limit on the permissible means that may be used to achieve some end, but the *legitimacy of the end* that is to be achieved and the *effectiveness* of the means in achieving the end: "A means," he says,

> can be justified only by its end. But the end in its turn needs to be justified. From the Marxist point of view, which expresses the historical interests of the proletariat, the end is justified if it leads to increasing the power of man over nature and to the abolition of the power of man over man. . . . That is permissible . . . which really leads to the liberation of mankind.[21]

When Trotsky speaks of a "dialectic interdependence of ends and means,"[22] he has in mind that not all means are permissible—only those means that *really* serve justifiable ends:

> When we say that the end justifies the means, then for us the conclusion follows that the great revolutionary end spurns those base means and ways which set one part of the working class against other parts, or attempt to make the masses happy without their participation; or lower the faith of the masses in themselves and their organization, replacing it by worship for the "leaders."[23]

The upshot is that there can be no "automatic answers" to "the question as to what is permissible in each separate case." In themselves, means are neutral. They gain their significance by reference to "objective expediency" rather than "subjective motives." The question to be asked is: "Are the given means *really* capable of leading to the goal?"[24]

Embedded in Trotsky's argument are at least two distinct issues: one concerns the efficacy of the means with respect to the ends pursued; the other concerns the legitimacy of the ends that are actually being pursued. (Trotsky appears to criticize Stalinism on both counts—on the one hand, by suggesting that the ends of the Stalinist regime are not really about the "liberation of mankind," but the consolidation of Stalinist power; and, on the other hand, by suggesting that Stalinist strategy is ineffective.)

When Dewey responded to Trotsky, he did not deny that the ends justify the means or argue that means must be constrained by "some form of absolutistic ethics based on the alleged deliverances of conscience, or a moral sense, or some brand of eternal truths."[25] Dewey took pains to note that ends may be of two kinds, intermediate and final and it is only the [most] final end that is justifying of the means—"that is, an end which does not need itself to be justified but is the justification of the ends that are in turn means to it."[26] Dewey agrees with Trotsky that the "increase of man's power over nature, accompanying the abolition of the power of man over man" might well constitute some such final end, though he is quick to point out that "others than Marxians might accept this formulation of *the* end and hold it expresses the moral interest of society—if not the historic interest—and not merely and exclusively that of the proletariat."[27] In other words, Dewey countenances the possibility that human emancipation may be a universal end, and not merely a sectional one (the end of the proletariat).[28]

The basis for Dewey's critique lies in his concern that means should be effectively tailored to their justifying ends. The recognition of the justifying end should, in Dewey's own words, lead to:

> scrupulous examination of the means that are used, to ascertain what their actual objective consequences will be as far as it is humanly possible to tell—to show that they do "really" lead to the liberation of mankind. It is at this point that the double significance of *end* becomes important. As far as it means consequences actually reached, it is clearly dependent upon means used, while measures in their capacity of means are dependent upon the end in the sense that they have to be viewed and judged on the ground of their actual objective results. On this basis, an *end-in-view* . . . is an *idea* of the final consequences, in case the idea is formed *on the ground of the means that are judged to be most likely to produce the end*. The end in view is thus itself means for directing action—just as a man's *idea* of health to be attained or a house to be built is not identical with *end* in the sense of actual outcome but is a means for directing action to achieve that end.[29]

There are two points here. One is the empirical point that the means should be such as to realize the end (or at least to make it highly probable that the ends will be realized). The second is that the end itself should provide guidance as to the means most likely to realize it. Dewey goes on to argue that, when Trotsky says that "dialectic materialism does not know dualism between means and end,"[30] "the natural interpretation is that he will recommend the use of means that can be shown by their own nature to lead to the liberation of mankind as an objective consequence."[31] But instead of "an examination of *all* means that are likely to attain this end without any fixed preconception as to what they *must* be,"[32] Trotsky "deduces a rule for conduct from the laws of the development of society, thus primarily from the class struggle, this law of all laws."[33] Thus, Dewey argues, "the principle of interdependence of means and ends has . . . disappeared or at least been submerged."[34]

For Dewey, it is only through empirical examination of what actually results from class struggle, and not by means of commitment to an ideology, that determines whether or not class struggle will be not only the means but the most effective means to the liberation of mankind.[35] Moreover, the way that class struggle is carried on will no doubt affect the sort of end to which it is directed.[36] So, Dewey concludes, means and ends are interrelated, and we need *evidence*, not *ideology*, for thinking that certain ends will be accomplished by the use of particular means.

Dewey's basic criticism seems well enough taken: one cannot foreclose the means by reference to a theory about historical development. George Novack offers a possible avenue of response by seeking to transform the laws of history into well-established historical generalizations.[37] Dewey, he writes, wrongly counterposes his inductive procedure to Trotsky's deductive one.[38] He accepts Dewey's point that the worth of conduct needs to be judged by its real consequences, but he argues that "the laws and needs of the class struggle . . . had been drawn from a prior comprehensive study of social processes over many generations by strictly scientific methods. The laws of class struggle are first of all *empirical* generalizations developed from analysis of the *facts* presented by the history of civilization."[39] He suggests that the prevalence and crucial role of class conflict in history were well known prior to Marx, but that Marx was the first to give a correct and adequate account of it.[40] And so, he concludes, Dewey fails to appreciate that some social judgments are so well grounded inductively that—like the laws of science—they allow us to make deductions from them: they have the status of laws.[41] I suspect that Novack has a far-too-sanguine view of the empirical character of such laws, but that discussion would take us too far afield.

The core of Dewey's argument is that "an *end-in-view* represents or is an *idea* of the final consequences, in case the idea is formed *on the ground of the means that are judged to be most likely to produce the end*."[42] The point here is that means do not exist in a realm of their own, waiting to be chosen for some end, but that when we choose or seek to realize an end, it comes with some idea of what will constitute appropriate means for its realization. That will involve a quasi-empirical examination of the kinds of means that are likely to bring the end about and, as well, a normative consideration of whether the means have features that will be compatible with the end or, on the contrary, are likely to undercut what makes the end valuable. (Clearly, the means may sometimes have effects that interfere with the achievement of the final end. For example, if the use of certain means to achieve an end is likely to alienate people from the end, then the means will diminish the likelihood of achieving the end. Moreover, the character of some ends may be so bound up with the means used to achieve them that the use of certain means will result in ends that are other than they were intended to be.)

Underlying Dewey's theory about the interrelatedness of ends and means is his view that the ends cast a normative light on the means that will be appropriate to their realization. To put it somewhat differently, many of the courses of action that can constitute means carry a normative, often moral, weight of their own, and this can either undermine the end or override it. Even if the end is important enough to justify the use of a problematic means, there may be another means that will accomplish the end at less normative cost, and if so we should choose the latter.

Of course, one may argue that one's final end is so important that no means should be ruled out a priori. However, even in such a case, we have to consider that some means, even in the case of very important ends, will be such as to undermine the very ends they are intended to serve. (In a "national security" initiative more than 40 years ago, designed to root out Communists by requiring a loyalty oath as a condition of employment, the US Supreme Court argued that "implicit in the term 'national defense' is the notion of defending those values and ideals which set this Nation apart." It then referred to the irony that would be involved "if, in the name of national defense, we would sanction the subversion" of those values that make "the defense of the Nation worthwhile").[43]

Another example—one that we will later (Chapter 8) explore in greater detail—is to be found in the discussion about the use of torture—and other forms of "enhanced interrogation." Focusing on the question whether harsh techniques are an effective means for educing terrorism-related information, some of the discussion has also concerned the compatibility of torture—whether effective or not—with the ideals of a liberal democratic society. In other words: does the inclusion of torture within the arsenal of the guardians of a democratic society erode its character as a liberal democratic society? (As we will also see, much the same kind of argument can be employed against the use of third-degree interrogational tactics in law enforcement).[44]

One of the problems with justifying means by reference to final ends is that the chain of means and ends is almost certain to be a long and complex one, easily subverted by unforeseen and unforeseeable contingencies. Therefore, the employment of means that are costly in moral and/or political terms must be very carefully weighed.

Concluding Remarks

If the value of means is simply instrumental, it may be questioned whether their being instrumentally valuable gives them *any* value of their own. As Monroe Beardsley expressed it, "being good as a means is not a way of being good—the instrumentally valuable thing is not a valuable instrument, strictly speaking, but an instrument of value."[45] Though there is something to be said for the truth of this, it may falsely represent the relation we have to many of the things that we view instrumentally—be they money, knives, or houses. These things have been brought into being not as instruments to serve single ends, but to serve us in a variety of contexts. We come to see them as being valuable in themselves *because* of the value they have in serving a variety of ends. Even if the good of a knife lies in the relatively limited function of cutting—such that we judge a knife largely by how well it cuts—we are desirous of cutting in many different contexts, and so knives are seen to be good things to have. Anyone setting out to furnish a house will want to have a set of knives, not because she has some specific end-in-view for which the knives will be instrumentally valuable, but because the instrumental value of knives has been made intrinsic to them.

Of course, that does not mean that a knife will always be an appropriate means to realizing an end, even if it is an effective means of realizing an end. Knives may be misused, as well as used.

Notes

1. M.K. Gandhi, *Young India*, 6 (July 17, 1924), 236–7; reprinted in *The Mind of Mahatma Gandhi*, R.K. Prabhu & U.R. Rao, rev. ed. (Ahmedabad: Jitendra T. Desai/Navajivan Trust, 1967), available at: www.mkgandhi.org/momgandhi/chap45.htm.
2. I ignore some more specialized understandings, such as that implicit in the phrase "a person of means"—where "means" refers to a specific kind of asset that allows the person a wide range of possibilities.
3. More remotely, though legitimately, something may be considered as a means because it is conceptually necessary to bringing about a certain end. If, for example, *X* wishes to marry *Y*, it may be conceptually necessary for *X* to employ a recognized marriage celebrant. Otherwise, any ritual that *X* and *Y* engage in (within a particular jurisdiction) will not function to accomplish the end of marriage. (Of course, if marriage is conceived differently, then this may not be considered a conceptual constraint. This hints at a further complication—whether, for example, something is thought of as conceptually necessary or only institutionally necessary.)
4. This is probably not true of a *lever*, which tends to be construed as something made and valuable for certain purpose, but might be true of a *stick* used as a lever. There is no implication that the stick has some inherent purpose (or value). For this account of conceptualization, see Julius Kovesi, *Moral Notions* (London: Routledge & Kegan Paul, 1967).
5. Talk of an end in itself does not require some metaphysical theory about the changelessness of its value or about its value independent of how the rest of the world is. All that needs be implied is that something is evaluable *apart* from its consequences. See A.C. Ewing, *The Definition of Good* (New York: Macmillan, 1947), 114. Cf. also Giuliano Pontara: "I believe that when people say that something is good in itself or for its own sake, what they actually mean is that the thing in question is good when considered apart from its consequences, but without meaning to say or imply that it is something good in exactly the same degree for all time to come and independently of the context in which it occurs," *Does the End Justify the Means? A Metaethical and Normative Study*, Filosofiska Studier, Häfte 20 (Stockholm: Filosofiska Institutionen vid Stockholms Universitet, 1967), 36. Pontara's study has been an extremely valuable resource in preparing this study; I have often drawn on the literature he cites.
6. Usually sourced to Gerald Seymour, *Harry's Game* (London: Hodder & Stoughton, 1975), 54. Its controversial character is explored in Boaz Ganor, "Is One Man's Terrorist Another Man's Freedom Fighter?," available at: www.ict.org.il/ResearchPublications/tabid/64/Articlsid/432/Default.aspx.
7. Cited in G.L. Kline, s.v. "Soviet Morality, Current," in *Encyclopedia of Morals*, ed. Vergilius Ferm (New York: Philosophical Library, 1956), 572; cf. George Leggett, *The Cheka: Lenin's Political Police* (New York: Oxford University Press, 1981). In this particular form, however, there is something conceptually problematic about the dependency claim, for normative considerations already distinguish murder, lies, and treachery from other forms of killing, saying what is false, and disclosure.
8. For a consolidated account of the debate, with texts, see Leon Trotsky, John Dewey, and George Novack, *Their Morals and Ours: Marxist Versus Liberal Views on Morality: Four Essays* (New York: Pathfinder Press, 1973).

9. He was assassinated in 1940 by Stalinist agents.
10. "Their Morals and Ours," in Trotsky, Dewey, and Novack, *Their Morals and Ours*, 20.
11. See, further, H. Gomperz, "When Does the End Sanctify the Means?," *Ethics*, 53 (1943): 173 n. 1. However, the "Doctrine of Double Effect" might be viewed as a sophisticated version of the view that the end justifies the means, and this would find Jesuit support. See Chapter 6.
12. "Their Morals and Ours," in Trotsky, Dewey, and Novack, *Their Morals and Ours*, 16.
13. Ibid., 17.
14. Ibid., 18.
15. Ibid., 19.
16. Referenced to *De scismate libri III* (1410), in *Darkness at Noon*, trans. Daphne Hardy (New York: Modern Library, 1941), 95. However, it has been argued that this is a somewhat inaccurate paraphrase by Ludwig von Pastor from another volume by Dietrich, *De modis uniendiae reformandi ecclesiam*, available at: http://en.wikipedia.org/wiki/Dietrich_of_Nieheim.
17. One view is that the individual is always an expression of a communal order of *some* kind and is therefore secondary to it. Another view is that the individual is in some sense dependent on the community, so that even though the individual has a certain moral primacy, if the consequences for the group are serious enough, individuals could be justifiably sacrificed for its well-being.
18. "Their Morals and Ours," in Trotsky, Dewey, and Novack, *Their Morals and Ours*, 32.
19. Ibid., 28.
20. Ibid.
21. Ibid., 40–1.
22. Ibid., 40.
23. Ibid., 41.
24. Ibid., 42.
25. "Means and Ends," in Trotsky, Dewey, and Novack, *Their Morals and Ours*, 56.
26. Ibid.
27. Ibid.
28. This is not a place at which Dewey expresses his usual worries about final ends and their connections with authoritarianism. Perhaps he felt that human emancipation was broad enough not to require a caveat.
29. "Means and Ends," in Trotsky, Dewey, and Novack, *Their Morals and Ours*, 56–7 (*emphasis in original*).
30. "Their Morals and Ours," in Trotsky, Dewey, and Novack, *Their Morals and Ours*, 41.
31. "Means and Ends," in Trotsky, Dewey, and Novack, *Their Morals and Ours*, 57.
32. Ibid. (*emphasis in original*).
33. "Their Morals and Ours," in Trotsky, Dewey, and Novack, *Their Morals and Ours*, 41.
34. "Means and Ends," in Trotsky, Dewey, and Novack, *Their Morals and Ours*, 58.
35. "the selection of class struggle as a means has to be justified, on the ground of the interdependence of means and end, by an examination of actual consequences of its use, not deductively" (ibid.).
36. There is more than one way in which a class struggle may be conducted: "How can a choice be made among these different ways except by examining their consequences in relation to the goal of liberation of mankind?" (ibid.). Seeking to hoist Trotsky on his own petard, Dewey suggests that "the belief that a law of history determines the particular way in which the struggle is to be carried on certainly seems to tend toward a fanatical and even mystical devotion to use of certain ways of conducting the class struggle to the exclusion of all other ways of conducting it" (ibid.).

37. Novack suggests that Trotsky was desirous of responding, but was prevented from doing so by "the press of other work" ("Liberal Morality," in Trotsky, Dewey, and Novack, *Their Morals and Ours*, 61).
38. Ibid., 67.
39. Ibid.
40. Ibid., 68.
41. Ibid., 68–72.
42. Trotsky, Dewey, and Novack "Means and Ends," in, *Their Morals and Ours*, 56–7.
43. *United States v. Robel*, 389 U.S. 258 at 264 (1967).
44. In addition, third-degree measures violate the Constitutional conditions for criminal conviction.
45. Beardsley, "Intrinsic Value," 5.

Chapter 4

Means in Policing

By any means necessary.[1]

Policing has, as a pragmatic occupation, its own temptations to excess. Police tend to have a firm idea of what they want to accomplish, albeit often cast too narrowly in terms of "catching crooks" or "enforcing the law." That desire may, by some, be suffixed with "by any means necessary" or implemented with a disregard for the quality of the means or their impact on the ends. As a result, police may violate privacy rights in order to gather information, they may allow a serious crime to occur in order to be sure to get a conviction, they may risk tragedy in order not to let a speeding driver get away, they may endanger others when the evidence does not warrant it, and so on. In defense, some police will echo the old military maxim: you can't make an omelet without breaking eggs.

I think we might agree that policing sometimes permits means that would otherwise be considered unethical. Yet one reason for being troubled by the kind of pragmatism referred to earlier is that it tends to ignore the wider moral, social, and political framework within which the end of policing is considered. Police are not simply charged with enforcing the law, but with enforcing it in the context of—and compatibly with—a particular social order. If the social order presents itself as a liberal democratic one, then liberal democratic constraints will—or at least should—infuse both the ends *and* the means of policing. To refer back to an earlier discussion, it is the fact that people are deemed to have certain rights whose exercise would be difficult in a state of nature that we can justify (and expect people to consent to) institutions with powers of the kind that we vest in police. If those constraints are ignored, then the raison d'être of policing is called into question.

Even if we expand the role of police in the way that I suggested in Chapter 2, and consider it to be one of social peacekeeping, that role needs to be understood in a particular way. In certain societies, social peacekeeping is better understood as social pacification or the enforcement of "social harmony," and police in these societies see their larger task as one of securing the regime in power. In the present discussion, what I understand by social peacekeeping is a peaceable social order in which fundamental rights are not merely acknowledged, but also championed.

Force

In a world that acknowledges human rights, and more particularly in a liberal social order, we place constraints on what humans may do to each other. Most centrally, we consider it prima facie wrong for human beings to use (unconsented-to) coercive force on one another.[2] Coercive force denies the right each of us has to determine our actions according to our own lights and thus be free from interference by others. Yet one of the things that most obviously distinguishes police from other citizens is the authority they are given to use coercive force. Usually they are armed—if not with firearms, then with batons, pepper spray, handcuffs, or tasers—and in appropriate circumstances, they are permitted to use these and other forms of physical force.

We noted earlier (Chapter 2) how this authority could be accounted for via the notion of a hypothetical social contract whereby reasonable people would see that the exercise of their fundamental rights would be maximized if they agreed to a civil order in which social norms were enforced via the creation of various social roles, including an executive power to ensure the maintenance of rights. Institutionalized policing constitutes one facet of that.

The exigencies of human social life as we encounter it necessitates the use of force. It may be necessary to prevent fundamental rights from being violated (say, by preventing someone from shooting an innocent other) or to interpose oneself in the event that others are being violated (by breaking up a brawl or intervening in an assault), or to ensure that those whom we have good reason (probable cause) to believe have violated the rights of others are made to answer for their crime (by making an arrest). As Locke recognized, human beings as we find them are not angels. More often than we might wish, they take advantage of others and cannot be relied upon to take responsibility for what they do or to make amends. Self-defensive and retributive coercive force may be used to secure those rights against invasion. The problem is that, individually, we are often not well placed to effect that permission. Hence, police and the other institutions of social order.

In our vesting in police the right to use coercive force, we do not of course give them the authority to use that force as they wish. It is a *constrained* authority—that is, an authority limited by the legitimate ends of the civil order that authorizes it. Police are expected to use (1) no more force than is necessary to accomplish their legitimate ends, (2) force that is proportionate to those ends, and (3) only the kind of force that makes it likely that their ends will be achieved.[3]

It is common to differentiate the police use of force as intermediate or deadly. For fairly obvious reasons, deadly force requires the more stringent justification, because it not only impinges on the freedom and bodily integrity of others, but also places their lives in jeopardy. It must therefore answer to a higher moral demand. What is more, it risks circumventing the legitimate limits of the police role, which is not to pass final judgment on the conduct of others, but to secure for judicial judgment the probably illegitimate acts of others. When police take it into their own hands to act as judge and executioner, they create the very failures that make the state of nature a rationally and morally unsatisfactory state of affairs.

At one point in the not-too-distant past, police were permitted—by what in common law was known as the fleeing felon rule—to use deadly force to prevent a suspect's escape from the scene of a felony. At the time the rule was established (several centuries ago), felonies were few and far between, and their seriousness was thought to warrant severe, if not capital, penalties.[4] But by the 1980s, offenses were usually categorized as felonies only if they attracted prison terms for longer than a year or death, thus rendering the fleeing felon rule a disproportionate response to attempts to avoid apprehension. In a major 1985 US Supreme Court case,[5] it was determined that only if a fleeing felon posed a serious danger to others was it justifiable to use deadly force to prevent escape. Thus was the fleeing felon rule brought under the wing of the "defense of life" rule (self-defense and defense of the lives of others being of long, and less controversial, standing).

As with deadly force, intermediate force needs to be both appropriate to the desired end and proportionate. It is not appropriate to use intermediate force as a form of punishment—punishment is for the courts, not the police, to determine.[6] And, like deadly force, intermediate force needs to be pitched to the need. Is it proportionate to bring an argumentative or passively resisting citizen into compliance by tasering her? Although many police departments promulgate use of force models or spectra,[7] they tend to focus on how much force might be permissible rather than on possibilities for de-escalation. (If anything has figured decisively in many of the incidents driving the #BlackLivesMatter movement, it has been the failure of police to employ tactics of de-escalation rather than those that aggressively assert control.)

To the extent that assertions of control are justified, they should be governed by a concern to inflict minimal damage. This is not to deny that using measures of "minimal damage" is without cost. Although physically and permanently non-injurious, such measures—say the use of pepper sprays, tear gas, or tasers—cause considerable pain and/or discomfort. And just as important, they create the possibility—perhaps even the temptation—for unjustifiable (and often unaccountable) overuse. Why argue with a person when she can be tased or sprayed? We should all be concerned that the lower the likelihood of "measurable" damage, and therefore accountability, the greater the likelihood that a particular kind of intermediate force will be abused.

Deception

Along with non-coerciveness in human relations, truthfulness is another value that is held in high regard within a liberal social environment. If the ground for the fundamental rights that humans have resides in their distinctive capacities, potentially and actually, individually and collectively, then included among these capacities is the ability to determine the course of their lives through the exercise of their own judgment. Humans are not cogs in machines; nor are they differentiated into those who rule and those who obey. They are (almost) all capable of self-determination, a capacity that depends crucially on the ability to assess the world for what it is, for that is the world within which self-determinative decisions take place. Although our individual capacities to engage in self-determinative decision-making may differ, we must presume that others to whom we relate will at least intend to be truthful in reporting on matters that are relevant to our own practical decision-making. If we cannot, that is likely to be crippling to our ability to be rational decision makers and actors. Lack of truthfulness, lying, and deception all constitute forms of assault on our status as rational, self-determining beings and, as such, show a deep lack of respect. We do not permit any lies—though obviously, we sometimes fail to prevent them—in the courtroom, for the court is the arbiter in matters of truth as those matters relate to just decision-making. The old English oath to "tell the truth, the whole truth, and nothing but the truth" is intended to ensure that witnesses, police or otherwise, pledge honesty to recount everything materially relevant, and not to include any known falsehoods.

Truthfulness in court, as elsewhere, has dignitarian value in acknowledging the respect due to others as rational determiners of the course of their own lives. But it also has utilitarian or instrumental value. Deceiving others often places them at unnecessary risk of harm. Truthfulness enables people to avoid such risks, or at least to take calculated risks for which they can then be held responsible.

Yet the principle of truthfulness is not exceptionless (despite some attempts to argue otherwise).[8] Although truthfulness acknowledges the high standing of others, and frequently diminishes the likelihood of harm, circumstances may arise in which it comes into conflict with other important values, and prioritizing judgments may need to be made. Most often, though not uncontroversially, the truth may be withheld—or even falsified—if telling the truth would place others in serious harm's way. Paternalistic deception (say, lying to a person about his/her medical condition) is often problematic if it makes unwarranted assumptions about the capacity of the other to handle it. But that sort of deception may also shield others from unwanted harms: Kant's notorious example of a potential murderer seeking the location of his intended innocent victim could be seen as the kind of case in which either a lying or deceptive response would be justified.

The exigencies of police work may well provide other occasions in which deception and lies may be justified. Undercover investigations and interrogations of suspects may allow for some—though not unbridled—lies and other forms of deception. Certainly with respect to criminal activity, contributors to that activity are not normally willing to be forthright about their involvement, and police may need to weigh both the possibility of using deception to get at the truth and the justifiability of using it on particular occasions.

Police are given no more license than others to engage in untruthful court testimony, but their investigative work is likely to provide circumstances for deceptive responses to situations. Most commonly, these may take the form of police hiding their identities in civilian clothing or in unmarked cars. Or they will engage in "sting" or other undercover operations. How far they may go in such deception is a matter of continuing contention. US courts tend to take a more liberal attitude to lying and deception by police than courts in England and Europe. For example, US courts may tolerate lies about evidence during interrogations that would be seen as legally impermissible elsewhere. Although there have been court cases in the United States dealing with police deception during interrogations, the ethical concern has mainly been with the *degree* of manipulation involved, and the likelihood that information obtained has verged on coerciveness. Suspects' vulnerabilities and fears may have been relentlessly exploited, or promises may have been made that police are in no position to fulfill. But there are wider ramifications, as well, ones of great social significance. To the extent that police activity becomes identified with deceptive practices, especially if those practices lack clear delineation, the public trust will have been jeopardized, a trust that is critical to police investigative and, more broadly, peacekeeping work.

In determining the acceptable limits to police deceptive practices, the ultimate question is (as with other facets of the civil order) whether the deception in which we authorize the police to engage would be agreed to by rational persons desirous of securing the exercise of their rights. At least in theory, if the police engagement in deception does a worse job of securing those rights than some alternative social arrangement, we will have sufficient reason to retract the authority that police have been accorded. And even if we do not withdraw their authority, we may, in light of their egregious use of that authority, decide to monitor and restrict it more than we currently do.

Invasions of Privacy

Police deception may not only impact on security, life, and liberty, but also on other important rights of personality such as privacy, dignity, and autonomy.

There has been an ongoing debate about the existence of a human right to privacy, and there have been corresponding debates about its nature, grounds, and limits. Although this study is probably not the place to deal with these issues in great depth, most of us will agree that there are kinds of information concerning ourselves whose disclosure should be left within our control. The right to privacy is closely bound up with the preservation of a personal space that is important to our moral autonomy. To the extent that certain kinds of information about ourselves is made available to others (without our knowledge or consent), our options for self-presentation and self-realization are diminished. Our lives become increasingly reactive to others' perceptions and expectations of us, rather than pro-active, in choosing to direct our lives as we wish. If non-chosen others are permitted to listen in on our private conversations, what we say and how we say it is moderated by the fact of their presence. (Even if we are not aware that non-chosen others are listening in, if there is no known normative barrier to their doing so, we must build into our communications the possibility that what we say is being overheard by parties other than our intended ones. Our decisions and communications are constrained by the possibility that others are listening in.[9])

As we have become increasingly aware, the recent boom in technology has made privacy a key and widespread social concern. Before modern technologies were developed, certain spaces—such as homes—were deemed loci of privacy. With technological developments such as telephones and personal computers, even private spaces have become vulnerable to intrusion (through the use of wiretapping, bugs, and malware). Now, with the explosion of cybertechnologies, the potential for intrusions into private space and the gathering of information over which we might reasonably expect to have control has placed in jeopardy a great deal of our self-determinative ability. Professional, social, and even intimate relationships, insofar as they depend on written or spoken communication, may be threatened, and information concerning ourselves, which we may wish to disclose only in limited circumstances, may be used to corrupt our social standing or otherwise to harm us. Computer hacking, GPS tracking, CCTV, and other technologies have placed great pressures on our ability to maintain as private that which we wish to remain private.[10]

Because of failures in human interactions (including our inability to resolve our differences), and the role we have given police to address them, access to private domains has become an important policing tool. Information gathering is critical to investigation, crime prevention, and responses to interactional failure. But as with force and deception, such access is open to misuse and abuse, and we have had to create limits that enable police to do their work without undermining the moral point of the whole policing exercise. When telephonic and recording technologies were introduced, police who wished to access an otherwise private domain were (and are) required to submit such invasions to judicial scrutiny and to apply for formal warrants. They are required to provide appropriate evidence (usually probable cause) for using a particular technology or in order to invade a private space. The complexities of social life and circumstances have made the actual rules governing police access quite complex, and a range of exceptions to regulative requirements have come to exist. Privacy law is a controversial work in progress.[11]

Reasons of security as well as hunches about criminal activity have been advanced for more mundane but no less egregious violations of privacy, such as the use of roadside or police station strip searches. A woman motorist in Florida was pulled over—allegedly for failing to come to a complete stop at a stop sign—and then strip-searched in public, while several male officers looked on and her children viewed the proceedings through the car window. To aggravate matters, the female officer who conducted the search removed the woman's tampon. No drugs or other contraband were found.[12] This was not an isolated case, and the issue has been exacerbated by a US Supreme Court decision allowing officers to strip search any person who is admitted to a cell, whether or not there is reason to believe that the person is carrying a weapon or contraband.[13] What made that decision even more problematic was the fact that the complainant in the triggering case was being confined as the result of a computer error about whether a fine had been paid. What might and should have led to a more nuanced decision was used to reinforce a police power that requires sensitive use, even when exercised on those who have been convicted of crimes. Justice Anthony Kennedy, who wrote for the 5–4 majority, fell somewhat short of the dignitarian impulses that infused some of his other decisions.[14]

In the next chapter, we will consider a range of questions that need to be addressed if we are to regard police exceptionalism as justified—questions about exemptions to moral duties regarding the use of force, deception, and invasions of privacy. What are important tools for police work need themselves to be constrained in certain ways so that the authority that we vest in police does not end up sabotaging the very rights that justify their authority. Police work, and the strategic options that are made available to police, cannot be justified by reference to some special ethics that police construct and observe, but by reference to considerations that we could *all* recognize as justifying what they do.

The Issue of Discretion

Linked to the foregoing prerogatives that give police exceptional powers is a more general police authority, that of using their own discretion to determine the ways in which they fulfill their professional role. Although liberal democratic societies are usually characterized as those bound by the rule of law—eschewing the personal arbitrariness of particular agents of a state—we nevertheless grant police (implicitly, if not explicitly) the authority to make discretionary judgments. This is not an uncontroversial authority. Some writers believe that, as agents of the law, any discretion that police have—at least so far as enforcement of the law is concerned—should be minimal,[15] though it is clear from studies of policing practice that police have always used a considerable amount of discretion.[16]

In saying that it is a prerogative, I am not suggesting simply that police have a license or freedom to make their own decisions, but *a right that we grant to them as a result of their professional role*. The prerogative that police have to use their own judgment is not the right or authority to do whatever they like, but a right, in certain circumstances, to make role-related judgments as seems to them most fit. They are professional and not simply personal or arbitrary judgments. For example, the discretion that a police officer has to give a warning rather than issue a ticket to a speeding driver, needs to be related to the *point* of policing (say, an acknowledgment of the offense, a suitable display of remorse, and promise to drive within the speed limit) rather than some other factor (say, the attractiveness of the speeding driver). Moreover, the recognition that the authority to exercise discretion is a right that police have only "in certain circumstances" is to recognize that the right is circumscribed in various ways. Police operate under departmental orders and rules, as well as under the law, and these may limit or expand their discretion in various ways. For example, orders or departmental rules may give police the discretion not to apprehend or ticket a driver who is driving less than 10% over the mandated speed limit, or they may *require* that police exercise discretion in the enforcement of litter laws when violators are very young, very old, or infirm. They may also permit officers not to arrest when a violator of marijuana laws is carrying only enough for personal use.

Problems that arise in the context of police discretion may concern its basis or its range. So far as the *basis* of police discretionary authority is concerned, the natural place to look is the ground for their authority in general—a ceding of some of our powers to certain civic officials in order that our rights in general are more reliably secured. But the rationale for allowing discretionary judgment on the part of police may not have the same facial plausibility in the case of police discretion as it has for police authority in general. The reason is that police authority in general derives from two other authorizations—one being a representative legislature that promulgates

> an established, settled, known law, received and allowed by common consent to be the standard of right and wrong, and the common measure to decide all controversies between them," and the other being a judiciary "with authority to determine all differences according to the established law.[17]

Put in more modern terms, police operate—or should operate—under "the rule of law;" they should ensure that the laws passed, interpreted, and applied are also enforced. "Discretionary authority" may look suspiciously like a subversion of the rule of law, and so it probably would be, were it not for a couple of factors.

First, police discretionary authority is not unbounded. Police are expected to make their discretionary judgments in line with their professional role. Second, police frequently operate in conditions of such uncertainty or complexity that rules—even clear-cut rules—cannot always accommodate general canons of fairness. Simple law enforcement is often a crude instrument of social control. For the most part, we do not cavil at the discretionary authority that police have—especially when it manifests itself, as it often does, in a more lenient application of the law than might have been allowed. It takes account of special circumstances, motives, and other factors that may have a mitigating effect.

This is not to deny that police discretionary authority may need to be monitored, and sometimes even constrained or altogether removed. Because police discretionary authority can come into conflict with the values that underlie the rule of law, there need to be ways for those who exercise discretionary authority to be held accountable. If, for example, more African-Americans are stopped and frisked or arrested for marijuana use (when apprehended) than white Americans, we may suspect that racial bias of some kind is at work. It does not, of course, necessarily follow that this is the case, but given the history of race relations as well as ongoing racial concerns, the possibility of bias needs to be confronted and addressed.[18]

As a general rule, the room for discretion is reduced as the probability of harm to others is increased. Safety is the major consideration behind rules creating speed limits, even though not every speeder poses a significant risk to others. Some people are quite capable of driving safely at speeds higher than the speed limit. However, a person visibly driving under the influence of alcohol poses a more significant risk to others, and a police officer charged with public safety has less discretion in how to respond to such a driver, making an arrest the default position. (An extremely problematic discretionary position was taken by British police a number of years ago, when making determinations whether to arrest in cases of parental child abuse. If the abuser was also the breadwinner, the police sometimes chose to warn rather than arrest in order not to jeopardize family economic functionality. There was good reason to think that arrests *should* have been made, and that ensuing economic problems should have been addressed in other ways.)

Problems about the *range* of police discretionary authority may encompass several distinct domains, which I broadly differentiate as those of (1) scope, (2) interpretation, (3) prioritization, and (4) tactics.

(1) *Scope* discretionary decisions on the part of the police concern judgments about whether an issue is of a kind with which police should involve themselves. Consider a dispute between neighbors concerning overhanging branches or the fruit thereon, the rescue of a cat from a

tree, a locked car, or the presence of garbage in the street. Police may not consider these as issues in which they should intervene—which is not to say that they should refuse to offer advice about appropriate resources for dealing with them. The boundaries of police social peacekeeping responsibility may vary with the size of a community and the divisions of labor that the community has established.

(2) *Interpretative* discretionary decisions focus on the way in which police might construe their involvement. Suppose a police officer stops to assist a stranded motorist, who then asks whom he should call for towing assistance. In some police departments, with a history of petty corruption, police may be prohibited from recommending towing services (to address a history of police kickbacks). If the police officer judges that the out-of-town stranger would have difficulty in finding a tow-truck operator, should he be prevented from recommending or even calling one (if the stranded motorist has no phone)? Rigid rule following in this case, as well as some others, may be counter-productive.

(3) Discretionary decisions about *prioritization* must mediate among what the police officer sees as pressing multiple demands. Police services are often stretched fairly thinly, and police must make decisions about where to direct their (greatest) attention. How much time should be given to the issue of jaywalkers or someone driving with a broken tail light when a reckless driver must be dealt with? Issues of social order and public safety are likely to press more urgently in such decision-making.

(4) Finally—and perhaps most importantly—police discretion often arises in the context of the *tactics or strategies* to be employed in their work. Such tactical decisions may arise at any point in their social peacekeeping activity—though often they arise most acutely at the investigative and interrogatory stages of law enforcement. Should police engage in a sting operation to catch certain law violators? If so, what should be the shape of such an operation, and what risks should they undertake? How should police proceed in a hostage situation, or when a mentally disturbed person creates a public nuisance? Most of these questions cannot be resolved by appeals to law or regulation, though law and regulation may provide some constraints on the actions that ought to be considered. For example, police may be prohibited from drawing their weapons unless certain conditions obtain, or they may have to follow certain procedures if they are to tap a telephone or enter into certain premises. Some decisions—say, concerning the use of tasers—may be restricted to persons of a certain rank or training.

Where police discretionary authority has a history of misuse or of being understood in conflicting ways, it is to be expected that formal constraints on its exercise will be developed—either through legislation, court determinations, or through departmentally promulgated rules. Such formal constraints will not, of course, remove all discretion—nor is it intended to. Rather, they will be adopted to limit it in certain ways so that problematic exercises of it will be minimized.

Conclusion

Because of the special challenges attending the police role, our authorization of their executive functions carries with it the permission to sometimes exceed boundaries that we ordinarily place on ourselves. Police have access to forcible means, permission to use deceptive practices, and permission to invade privacy. These exercises of discretion enable them to achieve for us what would have been at risk in a state of nature. Such moral extensions to their professional authority are not sui generis—grounded in a moral realm special to themselves—but are moral permissions that are grounded in society's need to secure the legitimate rights of its human members.

Nor are these extensions unbounded, but constrained in ways that minimize the failings of a state of nature and, in a liberal democratic order, do not undermine its commitment to the rule of law, but express the values that underlie it.

Notes

1. Wording included in a proposed bill permitting police to break up any protest that blocks a thoroughfare, Indiana Senate Bill 285 (Sen. Jim Tomes, January, 2017).
2. The situation is altered somewhat, though problematically, if there is consent. See John Kleinig, "Paternalism and Consent," in *Routledge Handbook on the Ethics of Consent*, ed. Peter Schaber and Andreas Müller (London: Routledge, 2018), ch. 13.
3. For a more detailed account of the limits to police use of force, see, John Kleinig, "Legitimate and Illegitimate Uses of Police Force," *Criminal Justice Ethics* 33, no. 2 (2014): 83–103.
4. According to Blackstone, a felony is "an offense which occasions a total forfeiture of either lands, or goods, or both, at the common law; and to which capital or other punishment may be superadded, according to the degree of guilt" (*Commentaries on the Laws of England* [1765–69], bk. IV, ch. 7), a far cry from its more recent understanding (in US law) as "typically a crime punishable by a term of imprisonment of not less than one year or by the death penalty" (Merriam Webster).
5. *Tennessee v. Garner*, 471 U.S. 1 (1985).
6. For a more fine-grained discussion of this point, see John Kleinig, "Punishment and the Ends of Policing," in *Liberal Criminal Theory: Essays for Andreas von Hirsch*, ed. A.P. Simester and A. Du Bois-Pedain (Oxford: Hart, 2014), 283–303.
7. Googling "use of force model" or "use of force spectrum," using the image option, brings up many examples.
8. Kant's views are notorious. See his essay, "On a Supposed Right to Lie from Altruistic Motives" (1797), available in various formats. For an effort to give Kant's position plausibility, see Christine Korsgaard, "The Right to Lie: Kant on Dealing with Evil," *Philosophy and Public Affairs* 15, no. 4 (1986): 325–49, available at: https://dash.harvard.edu/bitstream/handle/1/3200670/Korsgaard_RighttoLie.pdf?sequence=2.
9. Inter alia, George Orwell's *1984* (London: Secker & Warburg, 1949) depicts a world deprived of privacy.

10. In the United States, in particular, legal decisions have contributed to this situation.
11. For a more detailed discussion of this, see John Kleinig, Peter Mameli, Seumas Miller, Douglas Salane, and Adina Schwartz, *Security and Privacy: Global Standards for Ethical Identity Management in Contemporary Liberal Democratic States* (Canberra: ANU E Press, 2011), ch. 8, available at: http://press.anu.edu.au/publications/series/centre-applied-philosophy-and-public-ethics-cappe/security-and-privacy/download.
12. Donna Anderson, "Cops Strip Search Mom at Roadside, 'Forcibly' Remove Tampon While Kids Look On," Examiner.com, August 11, 2012, available at: www.examiner.com/article/cops-strip-search-mom-at-roadside-forcibly-remove-tampon-while-kids-look-on.
13. *Florence v. Board of Chosen Freeholders of the County of Burlington*, 566 U.S. 318 (2012).
14. The Court had access to data indicating the rarity of weapons and or contraband being found: Daphne Ha, "Blanket Policies for Strip Searching Pretrial Detainees: An Interdisciplinary Argument for Reasonableness," *Fordham Law Review* 79, no. 6 (2011): 2721–60.
15. See Jeffrey Reiman, "Is Police Discretion Justified in a Free Society?," in *Handled with Discretion: Ethical Issues in Police Decision Making*, ed. John Kleinig (Lanham, MD: Rowman & Littlefield, 1996), 71–83; "Against Police Discretion: Reply to John Kleinig," *Journal of Social Philosophy* 29 (Spring 1998): 132–42.
16. Samuel Walker, *Taming the System: The Control of Discretion in Criminal Justice, 1950–1990* (New York: Oxford University Press, 1993). I have discussed police discretion in greater detail in *The Ethics of Policing*, ch. 5. For an early bibliography on police discretion, see Susan L. Center, "Police Discretion: A Selected Bibliography," *Law and Contemporary Problems*, 47, no. 4 (1984): 303–12.
17. John Locke, *Second Treatise of Civil Government* (1689), ch. 9, available at: www.constitution.org/jl/2ndtreat.htm.
18. I have pursued the issue of bias at greater length in "To Protect and Serve: What Is Wrong with Policing of Minorities in the US?," *The Critique*, May 24, 2016, available at: www.thecritique.com/articles/to-protect-serve-what-is-wrong-with-the-policing-of-minorities-in-the-u-s/. It is arguable that concern about bias is one factor that lies behind the US rule that arrestees should be handcuffed. In many non-US police jurisdictions, a person who is arrested is informed of the fact and told to come with the officer for booking and further questioning. Handcuffing is discretionary and generally linked to judgments of dangerousness. Although other factors may be involved, there is a real possibility in the United States that handcuffing practices (along with stop-and-frisk practices) will be skewed by the racial identity of the arrestee—African-American arrestees being viewed as more dangerous than white arrestees.

Chapter 5

The Question of Justification

> An end which requires unjustified means is no justifiable end.[1]
>
> The end can morally justify the means only if the means does not morally disqualify the end.[2]
>
> Ordinarily, . . . both end and means come bundled together with the envelope of what we do.[3]

All of the foregoing comments about means raise questions of justification: Is the pursuit of particular ends justified? Is the use of a particular means justified? Is the use of a particular means justified *in relation to* a particular end? As the epigraphical quotations indicate, these questions are not questions of causal efficacy. Rather, they address deeply normative concerns.

I shall first offer some general comments on the nature of justification and then review the debate between those who argue that the ends can justify the means and those who reject such a claim. I shall suggest that the debate is sometimes stalemated by the failure to recognize that simple answers overlook a complexity of considerations that have to be taken into account.

Justification

What is it to provide a justification for particular actions and practices in which certain ends are pursued? How do we support the claim that engaging in certain actions or practices as a means to achieve certain ends is normatively acceptable? (No doubt, the justification we offer may appeal to certain beliefs that we have; but I am not here concerned with the justification of those beliefs, but rather with how those beliefs, assuming they are true—or at least well founded—justify actions undertaken as a means to an end.[4])

To give a justification is to give reasons. To give a justification for an action is not only to give *a* reason for doing that thing but to give a *good* reason (or set of reasons) for doing it. And because, in justifying our action or practice, we are claiming there is a good reason (or set of reasons) for our engaging in that act or practice, we can generally be said to imply that the reasons we give are sufficient for our acting in the way that we do. (Otherwise we might be more inclined to say that our reasons only partially justify our act, or simply contribute to the justification of our act. We will add some additional qualifications later.)

However, we should note the following. Sometimes when we give a reason for doing something, we are *not* seeking to show that the act is justified according to some acceptable normative principle, but are, rather, seeking only to explain what we did in terms of its causal antecedents. In such cases, we are not justifying our action, but merely (non-normatively) explaining it. Consider the differences between the following: (1) "I coughed because I wanted to draw attention to the fact that I was in the room" and (2) "I coughed because of a throat irritation." In (1), we are giving the reason *why we chose to act* in the way that we did; whereas in (2), we are citing the causal antecedent of our act and so implying that what we did was *not a result of our choice*. There are various distinctions we can draw between reasons and causes, but we will not go into them here. Sometimes explanatory, justificatory, and motivating reasons may overlap or even be identical. The important point here, however, is to note that justifications and explanations typically serve different functions: what explains how we come to engage in certain actions or practices (or what motivated us to engage in them) does not ipso facto constitute a justification for engaging in them.

Justificatory reasons are always normative. They attempt to show that what is, will be, or was done was the right thing to do. As a general rule, justificatory reasons are highly contextualized. Providing a justification of an act or practice is not ordinarily a matter of advancing *in abstracto* a set of good reasons for engaging in that act or practice. Rather, requests for a justification of what one did or is doing usually take place against the background of the belief or assumption that what one did or is doing is in some way faulty: it is morally wrong or irrational or—at the very least—uncalled for. (For this reason, there is a vast literature on the justification of the practice of punishment. Since punishment involves a negative imposition on a person—an imposition generally viewed as illegitimate—the justification of that imposition is rightly brought into question by the request that it be justified.)

On the account of justification that I present here, the request for a justification can be met in one of two ways. Either it can be shown that the act for which a justification is sought is *not deficient* in the ways suggested by the request for justification—say, my taking my neighbor's book was not in fact an act of stealing because she had given me permission to borrow it—or it can be shown that although the act was not faulty for that reason—say, I actually did steal the book from my neighbor, but I did so to prevent some great harm that would befall my neighbor were she to be found in possession of it.[5]

One consequence of this account is the relativity of justifications to the context in which requests for it arise. If Arthur satisfies Betty's demand for justification, he may not yet convince Camille, who has a different justificatory question. Or, Arthur may satisfy Betty for a time, but not for all time, as she may later present some new objection.

Consider a police case in which *A* is a high-speed chase that ends in an accident in which the person who was pursued is seriously injured. We might want to assume as a starting point that people who seek to evade police authority must expect to be pursued. But, someone asks, in the circumstances in question was Officer Abel justified in pursuing Barry Baker when the latter sought to avoid apprehension? It might be pointed out that high-speed pursuits are inherently dangerous and should therefore be initiated only in serious circumstances. It will then be for Officer Abel (or someone on his behalf) to show how the circumstances in Barry Baker's case were sufficiently serious to justify the risks involved in initiating or persisting in the high-speed pursuit. Suppose that demand is satisfied with respect to those who make it. New information may then emerge that casts doubt on whether the circumstances were as they were purported to be, or questions might be raised that were previously overlooked. In either case, the question of Abel's justification may be re-opened.

So far, we have noted that the idea of justifying a course of action involves removing whatever normative deficiencies have been imputed to it (by the request for a justification). What it *means* to "remove apparent normative deficiencies" with respect to an action (proposed, ongoing, or completed) is a question I shall leave open, for enough has been said to allow us to turn to the key question of whether the ends justify the means.

Do the Ends Justify the Means?[6]

It has probably now become clear that the general question, "Does the end justify the means?" is not amenable to a simple answer. As philosophers are inclined to say: it depends. Several considerations, none of which can be ignored and each of which needs to have a satisfactory response, bear on the answer to the question.

Given the variety of ends that we may seek, the variety of means that may be employed to secure our ends, and the variety of circumstances in which we must operate, it is not surprising that no single and simple formula will enable us to judge the legitimacy of using particular means to secure desired and desirable ends. There is no moral algorithm. Moral argument does not generally work like that: justification is an exercise of judgment, not the application of a formula. Nevertheless, in trying to determine the justifiability of a course of action or practice as means to a certain end, several important questions should be addressed regarding both the ends in question and any means that are contemplated or used to achieve those ends. *Each* of these questions needs to be addressed if we are to give any sort of affirmative response to the question: do the ends justify the means? Failure with regard to any one may negate an affirmative response.

Are the Ends Good or Good Enough?

As we noted earlier, ends come in many shapes and forms, and some ends are simply means to further ends. And even if they are more than that—even if the ends are, in addition, desired for their own sake—they may not constitute the kinds of ends that serve to justify the particular means that are used to reach them. What must be decided is whether the ends—either intermediate or final—possess sufficient intrinsic value to warrant the means in question. That is, the ends need to be deemed not only desired for their own sakes, but also desirable, and not only desirable, but desirable enough (perhaps taking into account as well any additional values they serve) to morally merit employing the means that are contemplated to bring about those ends.

Consider the following. A police officer aims to secure the legal conviction of someone he sincerely believes to be guilty of a crime, and decides, as police sometimes do, that he will "shade" his testimony to ensure that that person will be convicted. Securing the conviction cannot be a final—and therefore justificatory—end of the means employed unless the person believed to be guilty really *is* guilty (and even then it would not follow that any means will do). Furthermore, the conduct of which the person is believed to be guilty must be conduct that is legitimately criminalized (within, say, a liberal democracy). If, for example, one believes that the personal use of marijuana should *not* be criminalized, then one might be inclined to think that obtaining the legal conviction of a person guilty of possessing weed is not an end that justifies any effort that it takes to bring about that conviction (even though, legally, that may not be a matter for an individual police officer to determine). Furthermore, even if the offense *is* one that should be criminalized—it might still be questioned whether the offense is important enough to justify the use of the particular means used to bring about conviction for that offense. The means may be too heavy-handed or the resources required to ensure a conviction might be better employed elsewhere. In this vein, we might question whether police should be giving out summonses for jaywalking when there are more serious problems on the streets.

So, there needs to be a consideration of the worth of the ends one is pursuing. The ends are not simply "given," with the only normative issue being the means one might use to secure them. We therefore need to learn how to decide about ends, both intermediate and final. "The punishment of crime" or "the apprehension of criminals" may look to be important enough ends to justify certain kinds of police work. But if the criminalized behavior is not justifiably prohibited, this will not be so. The presentation of crime as a violation of important social or public norms looks good in the abstract, but its concretization in particular criminal prohibitions may leave considerable room for debate, a debate that will range as widely as the values that a liberal democratic society seeks to exemplify. It will also address whether a particular specification of criminal activity adequately serves the social norms that a liberal democracy seeks to uphold.[7]

Are the Means Proportionate to the End?

Although we may effectively get rid of a pesky fly with a shotgun, doing so would clearly be using means that are disproportionate to the task, for there are so many easier, less costly, and less dramatic but just as effective alternatives for achieving our aim.

However, the proportionality requirement is not simply a matter of efficiency or effectiveness. It runs deeper than this. When we speak of disproportionality between means and ends where humans are concerned, we often have in mind the idea of unfairness, the lack of a "moral matching" or fitness between means and end. For example, we may judge that the means are morally too extreme relative to the ends for which they are employed, say, using wiretaps—a drastic invasion of privacy—to catch the unwise admission of an occasional petty thief. So might be the construction of an elaborate sting operation that police have sometimes used—for example, sending letters notifying people of false lottery wins in order to lure them into custody—if employed simply to catch those who have failed to pay small parking fines. No doubt, some offenses warrant imaginative investigative strategies, but if these strategies are also used to catch those who are delinquent only in regard to parking fines, the means will almost certainly be excessive. Our reactions may be moderated, however, if each of the scofflaws has ignored thousands of dollars' worth of fines and the sting operation is designed to catch hundreds of such people at a time.

The proportionality requirement is frequently disregarded by police officers when it comes to the use of force. Whatever one's view may be of the legitimacy of handcuffing every arrestee—standard practice in the United States, though not in some other liberal democracies—the over-tightening of handcuffs is probably the most common disproportionate use of force. Whether used by a police officer in a retaliatory manner or as a way of his or her handling the adrenaline rush that often accompanies an arrest, it can be extremely painful, and even physically damaging. Much the same can be said for uses of force involved in apprehensions following high-speed pursuits. (Causes for the disproportionate use of force by police include not only the failure of the officer to deal with an adrenaline rush, but often also the sense that a person who seeks to avoid apprehension is showing disrespect for police authority, a disrespect that invites payback).[8]

Can the Ends Be Secured in a Less Invasive Manner?

Disproportionality offers one—but not the only—limit on police and other invasions. Another principle is that of the least restrictive alternative. In a liberal democracy, we place a premium on minimizing the extent to which people's liberty and other rights are compromised. Ends may often be achieved in more than one way and one means will sometimes be less costly, socially and individually, than others. Other things being equal, we should try to secure ends in the least restrictive way, even if what is an alternative way would not be disproportionate to the ends being secured. A strategic retreat might enable a situation to be handled more effectively ("Back down, not off") than a violent confrontation.

Suppose that a large demonstration is being planned and the police are concerned that it will get out of hand. They could turn out in great force, with riot gear, in an effort to deter or suppress "troublesome elements" in the crowd. Or they could meet with the organizers of the demonstration prior to its taking place in order to work out a *modus vivendi*. The demonstrators want to be able to make their point, and the police want to carry out their responsibility to ensure an orderly gathering. The police and organizers may be able to come to some prior agreement about how the rally will be organized—whether arrests are desired, how they will be handled, and so on—so that a less restrictive and more acceptable encounter occurs.[9]

It is the principle of the least restrictive alternative that drives the use of de-escalation techniques in police-citizen encounters. Although police have the authority (indeed, often an obligation) to intervene in socially disruptive situations, and may have the discretion to choose among various tactics for doing so, those tactics should be designed to minimize the extent to which others are imposed upon.

Will the Means Secure the Ends?

Means that are unlikely, or should have been known to be unlikely, to secure (even valuable) ends are means that are illegitimately used. Too often, we hear stories in which police, not having done their homework properly, have broken into apartments or apprehended individuals who have no connection at all with the legitimate purposes of police work.[10] Perhaps even more problematic are social policies that call on police to respond to certain situations but that show little likelihood of being successful. The "war on drugs" was a misguided attempt to stop the drug trade—misguided, because it failed (or refused) to come to terms with the social, economic, and psychological factors that drive the drug trade, and failed to see, therefore, that the punitive policies adopted were unlikely to dent it. That, of course, is not to sanction a laissez-faire approach to "the drug problem," but rather to suggest that certain ways of seeking to deal with it are likely to be unsuccessful and therefore wrong to pursue. Arguments for the deterrent effects of capital punishment, the usefulness of torturing terrorists, and recourse to profiling must confront similar challenges. My point here is not to suggest that, say, capital punishment could not be justified or that circumstances could never arise in which it would be excusable to torture a terrorist, or that profiling could never be a useful strategy, but that common beliefs about the usefulness of certain practices often lack empirical warrant.

Of course, in the real world of practical decision-making, success in achieving our ends by use of a particular means is almost always a matter of probabilities, and sometimes it is difficult to determine in advance what the probabilities of success are. Moreover, the importance of the ends will determine what *degree* of probability should be required before we are justified in proceeding. The more important our ends, the more we may be justified in proceeding with means that are less than certain to achieve these ends. The greater the goods that we aim at, the more we may not only be willing to risk in achieving them, but the more we will be justified in risking to pursue them.

Some might be prepared to argue that ceteris paribus, unless the end *is* achieved, the use of a particular means would not be justified. But that would be an excessive demand, for it would require that we wait until the means have been employed and the outcome of their use known before we can pass any judgment on the justifiability of the means. Usually we want to know not only whether what we *have done was justified* but also whether we *would be justified in going ahead* with some strategy, and this means making a judgment prior to our proceeding and therefore prior to our knowing whether our efforts will be successful.

It might also be argued that sometimes, even if we know (or have good reason to believe) that we will not be able to achieve what we are seeking, we are nonetheless justified in proceeding with our attempts.[11] Where a small country is attacked by a larger one and fighting back is unlikely to be successful, it may be that fighting back is still called for: rather than cave in (even to a hopeless situation), which would be degrading, it may be a matter of moral dignity to stand and fight a battle that one knows one cannot win. Or consider a case in which the search for a killer will consume vast resources with little likelihood of success: one might argue that out of respect for the victim and the victim's family, one should do whatever one can to try to find the killer, even if little is likely to be yielded by one's efforts to do so. What happens in these cases is that when an end is seen to be unattainable, we adjust our ends to something that is achievable and will nevertheless justify our continuing along the same path.

Is There Something Intrinsically Problematic About the Means?

Sometimes means may be chosen that are effective in achieving the ends that we are after, but are inherently problematic. Consider the following two examples, in which the end sought is unquestionably valuable but the means employed remain at best morally questionable and, most likely, morally unacceptable.

(1) A police undercover officer who, to gain information about an underworld figure, becomes intimate with a woman who has close connections with the person being investigated. The officer leads her to believe that he is in love with her and, in the course of the relationship, impregnates her. However, once he has exploited the relationship for whatever information he can get, he abandons her and vanishes. We may consider this an intrinsically unacceptable means to achieve the end of information gathering, because we believe that exploiting intimate relations, and particularly those that are likely to involve not only the abuse of intimacy but also long-term costs, is not to be countenanced for information-gathering purposes.[12]

(2) Government agents torture or otherwise treat inhumanely those whom they believe to have terrorist connections in order to gain information related to "the war on terrorism." Or, in the same context, government agents secretly and without court warrant subject citizens to comprehensive surveillance in order to obtain information that might be useful to them in their investigations. Since we consider torture and warrantless surveillance to be incompatible with our endorsement of the moral values of a liberal society, we will generally find these to be morally condemnable means (even if courts take a different view).

We will return to such cases later. The general point to notice, though—a point that we explored in the previous chapter—is that means are frequently not "morally neutral," that is, given value only by the ends to which they are directed. They often have a value in and of themselves, and in using them to secure some end, we must take into account any intrinsic *dis*value they have. The tendency to treat means as morally neutral has been a common failure in much political debate, where particular tactics are seen as unacceptable if "they" use them (since they are pursuing evil ends), but they are considered acceptable if "we" use them because we are pursuing good ends. This is also a pervasive challenge in policing, where deceptive and coercive means are frequently employed. (A case in point would be police illegally importing drugs on behalf of a distributor they are trying to apprehend.[13])

There are not too many absolutes in ethics. Intentionally killing the innocent, using the third degree on suspects, or torturing detainees may come close. However, the fact that situations can be envisaged under which most ethical values can be overridden—or their violations excused—leaves room for the possibility that even intrinsically bad means might, in the context of certain ends and in certain circumstances, be legitimately employed or excused. The hard question will be to determine the relevant threshold, and to prevent what we might call moral creep—a type of slippery slope in which we argue little by little from what might be permissible in an extreme situation to what can be permitted in less extreme situations. So common is it that moral possibilities are transformed into actualities by "social exigencies"—that it is often better to have total bans placed on some means than to allow them to be used in "special circumstances." The temptations for misuse are too great. We shall return to these issues in Chapter 8.

Will the Means Have Deleterious Consequences That Would Make Their Use Problematic?

An effective and otherwise acceptable means might run into moral difficulties if it has undesirable but unintended consequences.

Racial or ethnic profiling provides a salient, if controversial, example. If a particular racial or ethnic group is more heavily involved in drug running, human trafficking, or terrorism than others, it might seem a prudent use of resources to surveil and investigate members of that group more intensively just because they are members of the group predominantly involved in that activity. But doing so may have serious deleterious side effects. Because only a minority of members of the group is likely to be involved in drug running, it is therefore highly probable that a significant number of those investigated are innocent of any involvement. If we add—as we often can—that the group in question has been historically subject to social discrimination, then the profiling will tend to exacerbate their unfortunate social situation. Such was the experience of African-Americans who felt themselves "accused of" and harassed for "Driving While Black": they found themselves subject to suspicion that they were up to no good just because their skin color associated them with a group presumed to be more likely involved in criminal activity. Middle Eastern Muslims have confronted a similar prejudice since the events of 9/11.[14]

Much of the debate that surrounded the upsurge in stop-question-frisk in New York City a few years ago focused on the racial profiling that seemed to be involved in such decisions. Nearly 90% of cases resulted in no further action. At the same time, antagonism toward police was created or exacerbated. Police argued that without their aggressive monitoring of certain areas, crime would skyrocket, a claim that was subsequently shown to be baseless.[15]

I am not arguing against all profiling, even racial profiling. I am arguing that any profiling endeavor by police needs to be undertaken in a way that does not result in an abundance of false positives, and the socially problematic consequences that will accompany them.

Justifying Action

The foregoing questions—all of which need addressing and need to be answered satisfactorily—do not yield an algorithm for resolving means-end questions. Rather, they provide the basis for ethically informed judgment.

As I noted earlier, judgment is not a matter for formulaic calculations or for plus-and-minus columns, but rather an argumentative exercise in which various considerations, both normative and empirical, are brought into play and determinations made about their relative importance vis-à-vis each other. This can sometimes be a lengthy process, something like a jury seeking to come to a consensus with a range of considerations before it. And, also like a jury, conclusions may be associated with a range of probabilities. Unlike juries (at least in criminal cases) there is no "beyond reasonable doubt" standard that must be satisfied. Civil decisions, with their "preponderance of evidence" standard, may be closer to the mark, though situations must be accommodated in which it remains unclear whether either particular ends should be pursued or means adopted. Decision-making in police work must frequently occur under conditions of uncertainty. And, as in the case of "dirty hands" situations, to be discussed in Chapter 10, decisions must sometimes be taken that will leave moral residues. In such cases, we need evidence that the judgmental process was at least taken seriously and not short-circuited.

Consider a case in which police are engaged in an investigation of possible terrorist planning. At what point do they intervene or decide that the situation does not warrant further investigation? How much evidence will they need to have to satisfy a court of law? How much potential risk for innocents should they countenance before having sufficient reason to move? What kinds of surveillance are they justified in using, given their uncertainties and also given the possibility of compromising their investigation? Each of these questions (and probably others) needs to be addressed, and police need to be able to show and defend the kind of reasoning they used in reaching some answer on them.

Too often our judgments are corrupted by poor reasoning—by thinking too fast and not deliberately enough.[16] Over a lifetime of research, Daniel Kahneman (initially with Amos Tversky) has identified a number of ways in which our ordinary thought processes are subject to cognitive biases which distort our judgments. Originally designed to expose the failures of so-called economic rationality, a paradigm of means-end reasoning, Kahneman and Tversky's work drew attention to the ways in which reasoning—even if focused on the several questions I have developed in this chapter—could nevertheless be derailed. Hence the need not only for such questions to be addressed, but the ways in which, once addressed, they were judgmentally brought together.[17]

One other lesson from the foregoing discussion should also be clear. Although means-end reasoning often presents itself as consequentialist—that is, as though the issue is simply one of maximizing the likelihood that certain ends will be achieved—much more is involved. Means may carry a moral weight of their own that stands in tension with the pressures of maximization. There are various ways to see this. One philosophical debate relevant to this issue concerns the sacrifice of some lives to save a greater number.[18] Here there is something about the means—the using of a person merely as a means—that rules out that kind of option. What that might be, we shall explore in Chapter 7.

A related debate invokes the Blackstonian maxim: "It is better that ten guilty men go free than that one innocent man is convicted."[19] Although the maxim attracts contrary responses and competing justifications/refutations, almost certainly there lies behind it a non-maximizing impulse.[20] Although there may be an unjustified stringency in the various ways the maxim is formulated (what if the ratio were 1000:1?),[21] the preference for ensuring that the innocent aren't victimized by the system is not simply a matter of numbers.

Conclusion

The significance of the foregoing discussion for policing decisions should be clear, especially as the impact of such decisions on others may be considerable. A world that has a tendency to see itself in terms of "us-versus-them," that is prone to self-justification, that often makes decisions under conditions of uncertainty, and that must often respond rapidly to situations, is also one in which decisions are likely to be fast rather than slow, and therefore ones in which various cognitive and other biases are not recognized, and so fail to be corrected.

Notes

1. Karl Marx, "[Censorship]," Proceedings of the Sixth Rhine Province Assembly, on Freedom of the Press, Originally Published in *Rheinische Zeitung*, no. 135 Supplement (May 15, 1842), available at: www.marxists.org/archive/marx/works/1842/free-press/index.htm.
2. Svetozar Stojanović, "Revolutionary Teleology and Ethics," trans. from "Revolucionarna Teleologija i Etika," and printed in *Tolerance and Revolution: A Marxist-Non-Marxist Dialogue*, ed. Paul Kurtz and Svetozar Stojanović (Beograd: Philosophical Society of Serbia, 1970), 29–48, at 31, available at: www.autodidactproject.org/other/tolerance_revolution/stojanovic.html.
3. Henry S. Richardson, *Practical Reasoning about Final Ends* (Cambridge, UK: Cambridge University Press, 1994), 61.
4. The two are, of course, related. We might say that what we are looking for is the justification for believing that certain actions or practices are or will be justified.
5. This is probably to be seen as a coherentist theory of justification. There are many competing views—externalist, foundationalist, and so forth. For useful entrées to this issue, see the various articles included in the online *Stanford Encyclopedia of Philosophy* (https://plato.stanford.edu/): Erik Olsson, "Coherentist Theories of Epistemic Justification"; George Pappas, "Internalist vs. Externalist Conceptions of Epistemic Justification"; and Ali Hasan, "Foundationalist Theories of Epistemic Justification."
6. I have offered some preliminary responses to this question in *Ethics in Criminal Justice: An Introduction* (Cambridge, UK: Cambridge University Press, 2008), ch. 3.

7. Of course, in a wider debate, even a particular specification of liberal democratic values might be challenged.
8. For greater detail, see "Legitimate and Illegitimate Uses of Police Force," 6–9.
9. The difference between the matters of proportionality and invasiveness can be illustrated by means of the following hypothetical. Suppose that I am being pursued by a gunman who is trying to kill me. A proportionate response on my part would be to try to shoot the gunman so as to avoid being killed by him. Were my shooting the gunman not only to incapacitate him but also to kill him, my killing him would be considered a proportionate (self-defensive) response. But suppose I notice that there is a doorway between the gunman and me that I can escape through so as to avoid his pursuit of me. Since my escape would be the less invasive response on my part, it is the one advocated by the principle of the least restrictive alternative. To iterate: in the case described, killing the gunman would be a proportionate response, but escape would be the least restrictive or invasive alternative—and so the preferred response.
10. For one recent case, see Kristin Rodine, "Boise Police Break into Wrong North End Apartment to Serve Search Warrant," *Idaho Statesman*, 6/17/2015, available at: www.idahostatesman.com/news/local/crime/article41561151.html. The increasing use of SWAT teams to accomplish such ends—itself an often questionable strategy—has sometimes resulted in tragic outcomes. See Vicki Brown, "Man Dies in Police Raid on Wrong House," ABC News, July 19, 2017, available at: http://abcnews.go.com/US/story?id=95475&page=1; Mitch Ryals, "Sheriff's Deputies Search Wrong House, Tell Innocent Man He's Lucky Not to be Shot, Then Lose in Court," *Inlander*, 6/29/2017, available at: www.inlander.com/Bloglander/archives/2017/06/29/sheriffs-deputies-search-wrong-house-tell-innocent-man-hes-lucky-not-to-be-shot.
11. The traditional theory of war says that one is not justified in fighting back unless there is some likelihood of success. This is questionable, though whether we might have a duty to resist is also unclear.
12. For an extended discussion, see Gary Marx, "Under-the-Covers Undercover Investigations: Some Reflections on the State's Use of Sex and Deception in Law Enforcement," *Criminal Justice Ethics* 11, no. 1 (Spring 1992): 13–24,. A later revision can be found at: http://web.mit.edu/gtmarx/www/undercovers.html. The courts have been less protective of disclosures arising out of intimate relationships: *Hoffa v. United States*, 385 U.S. 293 (1966).
13. This was a problem in an Australian case, *Ridgeway v. The Queen*, (1995) 184 C.L.R. 19. The legislature subsequently responded by making an exception of government agents in sting operations. It is, however, arguable that the original law was written too narrowly.
14. There is considerable irony in this, as, by 2000, it was generally agreed that the profiling of African-Americans had been disastrous and unjustified. But immediately after 9/11, all this seemed to be forgotten as those who appeared to satisfy a "Middle Eastern" Muslim appearance were subject to discriminatory profiling, often with disastrous consequences. The courts, unfortunately, have been unpersuaded by the case presented by those discriminated against, appealing instead to the Ciceronian dictum: "Laws are silent when arms are raised" (*Silent enim leges inter arma*: M. Tulli Ciceronis (c. 106–43 BCE), *Pro T. Annio Milone ad iudices oratio*, intro. and comm. Albert C. Clark [Oxford: Clarendon, 1985], 10). See the recent case of *Ziglar v. Abbasi, et al.* (Slip Opinion, No. 15–1358, October Term, 2017), available at: www.supremecourt.gov/opinions/16pdf/15-1358_6khn.pdf, in which victims of discriminatory official treatment post-9/11 unsuccessfully argued for standing to pursue compensatory claims. In dissent, Justice Steven Breyer correctly but unpersuasively argued: "History tells us of far too many instances where the executive or

legislative branch took actions during time of war that, on later examination, turned out unnecessarily and unreasonably to have deprived American citizens of basic constitutional rights."

15. See, for example, John Cassidy, "The Statistical Debate Behind the Stop-and-Frisk Verdict," *The New Yorker*, 8/13/2013, available at: www.newyorker.com/news/john-cassidy/the-statistical-debate-behind-the-stop-and-frisk-verdict; Andrew Gelman, Jeffrey Fagan, and Alex Kiss, "An Analysis of the New York City Police Department's 'Stop-and-Frisk' Policy in the Context of Claims of Racial Bias," *Journal of the American Statistical Association* 102, no. 479 (2007): 813–23; Dylan Matthews, "Ray Kelly Says Stop & Frisk Saves Lives: There's No Good Evidence for That," *Washington Post*, 8/20/2013, available at: www.washingtonpost.com/blogs/wonkblog/wp/2013/08/20/ray-kelly-says-stop-frisk-saves-lives-theres-no-good-evidence-for-that/.
16. See, for example, Daniel Kahneman, *Thinking Fast and Slow* (New York: Farrar, Straus and Giroux, 2011). Our thinking is also corrupted by normative implicit biases. See, for example, Michael Brownstein, *The Implicit Mind: Cognitive Architecture, the Self, and Ethics* (New York: Oxford University Press, 2018).
17. For an application of Kahneman-type observations to the prosecurorial process, see Mark Godsey, *Blind Injustice* (Oakland, CA: University of California Press, 2017).
18. There are numerous versions of this argument. See the large follow-up discussions of John Harris, "The Survival Lottery," *Philosophy* 50 (1975): 81–7; "Jim and the Indians," an example used by Bernard Williams in J.J.C. Smart and Bernard Williams, *Utilitarianism: For and Against* (Cambridge, UK: Cambridge University Press, 1973), 98–9; Philippa Foot, "The Trolley Problem," *Oxford Review* no. 5 (1967); John Taurek, "Should the Numbers Count?," *Philosophy & Public Affairs* 6, no. 4 (1977): 293–316. Although some of the discussion in some of these cases is directed to the moral relevance—if any—of the distinction between killing and letting die, they also raise the issue of the adequacy of bottom-line maximizing thinking.
19. William Blackstone, *Commentary on the Laws of England*, 21st ed. (1765; London: Sweet, Maxwell, Stevens & Norton, 1844), bk. IV, ch. 27, p. 358. See, e.g., Alexander Volokh, "*n* Guilty Men," *University of Pennsylvania Law Review* 146 (1997): 173–211, available at: https://scholarship.law.upenn.edu/cgi/viewcontent.cgi?article=3427&context=penn_law_review.
20. For a useful debate, see Jeffrey Reiman and Ernest van den Haag, "On the Common Saying That It Is Better That Ten Guilty Persons Escape Than That One Innocent Suffer: Pro and Con," *Social Philosophy and Policy* 7, no. 2 (1990): 226–48.
21. Consider the problems associated with an alternative maxim: "Let justice be done, though the heavens fall"—*fiat justitia ruat caelum*—originally intended to be taken at face value by Lord Mansfield, in *Somerset v. Stewart* (1772), 98 ER 499), but now often seen as a *reductio ad absurdum*.

Chapter 6

The Doctrine of Double Effect

> Nothing hinders one act from having two effects, only one of which is intended, while the other is beside the intention. Now moral acts take their species according to what is intended, and not according to what is beside the intention, since this is accidental. . . . And yet, though proceeding from a good intention, an act may be rendered unlawful, if it be out of proportion to the end.[1]

We have already made some mention of the Doctrine of Double Effect (DDE), a doctrine that offers a subtle, if somewhat controversial, variant on the discussion of the previous chapter. The DDE usually has as its background the presumption that intentionally causing certain harms—e.g., killing those whom we know to be innocent—even as means of bringing about proportionately good ends, is absolutely wrong. The DDE builds on that presumption to provide an "exception." This exception has its roots in Catholic theology (especially in its Thomist variety; see the epigraph), although some (non-absolutist) versions of the doctrine have subsequently been more widely articulated and supported.

Scope

As to the exact formulation of the doctrine, there has been considerable dispute. In what follows I rephrase a popular statement of the doctrine associated with Joseph Mangan:

It is morally permissible to perform an action that one knows will produce not only a good effect but also a bad effect, so long as the following four conditions hold true:

1. that the action in itself from its very object be good or at least indifferent;
2. of the two effects that will be produced by the action, it is the good, and not the bad, effect that one intends to produce;

3. that the good effect produced by the action not be brought about as the result of the bad effect; and
4. that there be a proportionately very serious reason for doing what one knows will eventuate in a bad effect.[2]

The foregoing formulation (or something like it) has struck many people as capturing an important truth about the conditions under which it is morally permissible—even if not morally optimal—to pursue certain ends despite the fact that we know that their pursuit will produce certain bad effects. That truth is commonly illustrated by appeal to (what is held to be) a morally significant distinction between the following cases: (1) Although he can avoid the confrontation, *A* intentionally kills *B*, because he knows that *B* is trying to kill him; and (2) Knowing that *B* is trying to kill him, *A* takes steps to stop *B* but, given the available means for *A* to stop *B*, *A* realizes that what he does will probably result in *B*'s death. It is held that in (1) what *A* does is morally wrong, whereas in (2), what *A* does is morally permissible, the moral difference between these cases resting on whether or not the killing of *B* was intended or merely foreseen. In (1), *B*'s death is intended, whereas in (2), *B*'s death is merely foreseen.

Another pair of hypotheticals, much favored in philosophical circles,[3] is the following: (3) *A* sees that a runaway car will plow into and kill a group of five people in its path if the car is not stopped before reaching the group. *A* can stop the car by pushing a person in front of it, though, of course, the person whom he pushes into the path of the car will himself be killed; (4) as before, *A* sees that a runaway car will plow into and kill a group of five people in its path if the car is not stopped before reaching the group. *A* realizes that he can save the five people towards whom the car is headed by diverting the car onto a different path, albeit one on which there is a person who will not be able to get out of the way in time and who will therefore be killed by the diverted car. Here again there is claimed to be a moral distinction between the two cases. In (3), *A* is held to be guilty of moral wrongdoing because he intentionally pushes a person to his inevitable death. (4) is (often) held to be a case in which what *A* does is morally permissible (albeit regrettable) because, in diverting the runaway car onto a path on which a person is standing, it is not intended by *A* that the person be killed even though *A* may well foresee that this will be the result of his diversionary action.

Another commonly appealed to example involves morally differentiating between: (5) one's intending to blow up an enemy's critically important munitions dump, even though it is clearly foreseen that a side effect of that action will be the destruction of a nearby school and the (regrettable) killing of all its pupils; and (6) actually targeting the school and its pupils, where a foreseen consequence will be the destruction of the munitions dump.[4] Is (5) morally permissible and (6) morally impermissible? It is often thought so.

DDE reasoning is most often employed in criminal law contexts, especially where the death of some innocent person is said to be involved: (7) at the beginning of life, those who oppose and sometimes wish to criminalize abortion (as intentional killing of the newborn) often make an exception in cases of, say, ectopic pregnancies or uterine cancer, in which an operation to save the mother will have the death of the fetus/unborn as a regrettable side effect; (8) at the end of life, administering large doses of morphine is sometimes justified on the grounds of pain relief, even though the respiratory consequences will foreseeably be fatal, thus distinguishing it from (outlawed) euthanasia.

The point in each of these cases is that what would otherwise be a morally impermissible act (the killing of an innocent human being) is held to be brought within the bounds of moral permissibility, because it is not the intended but only the foreseen ancillary (i.e., "double") effect of one's intentional act. Thus, the designation "Doctrine of *Double* Effect": when acting intentionally to produce an effect that constitutes a clear moral good, the consequential production of another effect, foreseen but not intended—that is, a double effect—is morally permissible, even when that other effect is morally regrettable.

As one might expect, not everyone is persuaded by the judgments that go with the aforementioned contrasting cases. Some would oppose even the supposedly permissible alternatives, and others would come to different judgments from those proposed. For others, "it all depends," where what it depends on is some other factor that first needs to be resolved. The absence of clear or at least commonly accepted intuitions makes it difficult to use the cases to tease out underlying differentiating principles.

As noted, acceptance of the Doctrine of Double Effect—that ceteris paribus, we may do what is otherwise morally wrong if it is comes about as a result of our pursuing some clear moral good—is not universal. Its persuasiveness depends upon the details of the particular case we are looking at. Still, it is often used in making moral judgments about police work, where it focuses on the kinds of intentions that police have when seeking to pursue their ends, and proportionality between those ends and the means police choose to bring about those ends. Consider a high-speed chase in which police seek the good end of apprehending a high-value suspect. Suppose, too, that a possible consequence (here a matter of probabilities) will be an accident involving the police or the pursued person in which innocent persons will be injured or killed. How shall we assess the morality of such a high-speed chase? No doubt, a key factor will be the "value" of the suspect to the police. Clearly, engaging in a high-speed chase (with its attendant risks) to apprehend a simple traffic violator won't do. But what about the police pursuit of someone believed to be a dangerous terrorist?

Sherry Colb is one writer who has made explicit appeal to DDE a way of illuminating some of the debates surrounding the US Fourth Amendment exclusionary rule, which constrains government agents (including police) from conducting searches and seizures that are deemed "unreasonable."[5] She begins by claiming that one of the unfortunate consequences of the Fourth Amendment, and in particular its exclusionary rule interpretation, is that the amendment's deterrent effect inhibits police from intervening in ongoing and planned crimes and thus enables some guilty persons to go free. Even if there is support for the amendment, it is sometimes argued that the exclusionary interpretation is too demanding, and efforts have often been made to diminish its impact or even to abandon it.[6]

By barring government agents from unreasonable searches and seizures, the Fourth Amendment, especially given its exclusionary rule interpretation, lowers the likelihood of apprehending people who are guilty of criminal conduct. No doubt, it can be argued that the Fourth Amendment per se can pass DDE muster because we would complain about disproportionate consequences were police not constrained in some way in going about their law enforcement work. There would be a disproportionate threat to our security and liberty were police unconstrained, even though those constraints will have the effect of enabling some to engage in criminal behavior and get away with it. So, writes Colb, in deciding to support the Fourth Amendment, we pursue a good end—namely, securing our privacy and liberty—even though the cost will be a bad effect, albeit one that is not intended or even required as a way of securing that privacy and security (we do not let criminals go free as a way of securing our liberty—it is simply an unfortunate contingent side effect).

According to Colb, when we move from the Fourth Amendment to its exclusionary rule interpretation, the problem is made most acute, and the DDE argument becomes more controversial. For here, she says, the bad effect becomes direct instead of incidental:

> We are no longer prohibiting the police from performing unreasonable searches and seizures with the *knowledge* that guilty people will remain free as a result; we are directly subverting the truth-finding process in a criminal case by taking evidence that we already have, and refusing to allow the prosecution to present that evidence to the jury.[7]

True, any Fourth Amendment regime will require some enforcement mechanism—whether civil liability, judicial discretion, or something of that kind. But in such cases, the expectations of the doctrine could be met on both proportionality and privacy protection grounds. The exclusionary rule, however, "intentionally impedes a criminal prosecution by keeping probative evidence from a jury and does so as a *means* of deterring future violations."[8] If she is right about this, it might help to explain (1) why the exclusionary rule interpretation of the Fourth Amendment is so controversial (even if the Fourth Amendment is not), and (2) why the approaches of some other democratic countries to what are in effect Fourth Amendment violations differ from that of the United States.

In the end, Colb thinks that dismantling the exclusionary rule would be a mistake because, she writes, the benefits of having the rule outweigh its drawbacks, considerable though these drawbacks are. She argues that if evidence that police have gathered by illegal means is prevented from being presented in court, it will put police on notice that if they obtain evidence through illegal means, the evidence will have no probative value. In the end, we may do better with a strong rule than we would with a weaker or discretionary rule—although whether that is so is obviously a matter for some form of empirical inquiry.

If Colb is correct in thinking that that the question of whether we should or should not have exclusionary rules regarding the collection of evidence in criminal cases is ultimately a question of whether the intentionally pursued goods do or don't outweigh the negative ancillary effects of that pursuit, there still remains the question of whether the Doctrine of Double Effect itself captures an important moral distinction, one that can be fruitfully appealed to in criminal justice contexts. Moreover, even if the Doctrine of Double Effect highlights a moral distinction that *is* important to make, we still have to question the relevance and importance of that distinction in each and every case.

Underlying Rationales

Formulating what it is that gives the Doctrine of Double Effect the weight that it appears to have has constituted an ongoing challenge for philosophers, lawyers, and, one might suggest, criminologists. This may not be the place to attempt to resolve that challenge decisively, but there is some value in indicating and assessing considerations that are relevant to the case.

A key issue in much of the debate about DDE has been the distinction between a bad or evil effect that is intended and one that is merely foreseen but not intended. Is there a clear distinction between the two, and, if so, is it morally significant? So far as the former question is concerned, there are problem cases. Glanville Williams famously argued that we are unlikely to be impressed if a person who blows up a passenger aircraft in order to collect the insurance then argues at a murder trial that the passenger deaths were only foreseen and not intended.[9]

Nevertheless, we should not allow such cases to undermine the validity of the distinction or our capacity to make it. Equally famously, H.L.A. Hart argues that it would be misleading to claim that prisoners who sought to escape a POW camp but considered their chances of success close to zero could be said to intend and not merely foresee their failure.[10] Hard cases should not prevent us from making a conceptual distinction. When we intend an outcome, we commit ourselves to it and take steps to ensure it.

When we only foresee an outcome, we do not commit ourselves to it or take steps to bring it about (even if we can see that the steps we take will increase the probability that it will come about).

The ability to draw a distinction, however, does not resolve the moral issue; namely, its ethical significance. The moral difference between intending a bad or evil outcome and merely foreseeing it is not obvious to everybody. Those who ground moral assessments in outcomes, as consequentialists are inclined to do, may also be tempted to argue that if there is any difference between the two, it is only because an intended bad effect is more likely to come about than a merely foreseen bad effect, but that—insofar as what is foreseen is identical to what is intended—they are morally indistinguishable. Such people will not be persuaded that there is a significant moral difference between cases (5) and (6) earlier in this chapter, in which a successful bombing mission intends the deaths of the schoolchildren (6) and one in which their deaths are simply foreseen (5). They will argue that moral grounds for any differentiation will have to lie elsewhere.

This ultimately forces us to consider what we take morality to be—whether we think of it simply in terms of certain impacts that our conduct has on others (or ourselves), or whether (and how) it also involves the attitudes, intentions, and emotions that inform our conduct, whether that affects others or only ourselves. My own view here is that morality is fundamentally concerned with our relations with others (not excluding ourselves) in virtue of our capacities (emotional and otherwise) and the claim that they make on how we act. We often speak of the dignity that humans possess or the respect that is due to others by virtue of their capacities for thinking, feeling, and decision-making. This is not a simple matter of the consequences of what we do to each other, but of having a certain regard for them. Even that paradigmatic defender of consequentialist thought, John Stuart Mill, when avowing that he took "utility as the ultimate appeal on all ethical questions," quickly qualified it as "utility in the largest sense, grounded on the permanent interests of man as a progressive being."[11] And that, as Chapter III of Mill's *On Liberty* makes clear, involved an expansive and decidedly non-utilitarian understanding of persons.

No account of morality is entirely unproblematic, but its central feature—namely, that assessments of human interaction should not be seen simply as a function of outcomes, but also of the attitudes and intentions that inform those outcomes—is, I think, strongly indicated. If I accidentally hurt you, or negligently hurt you or intentionally hurt you, that counts for something, not simply in terms of the probabilities of your being hurt, its magnitude, and what should be done to minimize it, but also in terms of what kind of a person I am in hurting you. Ordinarily *intending* to hurt another is morally differentiable from doing something that brings it about without aiming at it. This is not necessarily to relieve someone of all responsibility for hurting another. Hurting others negligently may also incur judgment and blame, though not usually the kind of blame that goes with what the lawyers refer to as mens rea, or an evil mind.

The distinctions between intending to hurt another and unintentionally doing so or even foreseeing doing so may not always have moral significance, and there will be a need to distinguish those cases in which the distinctions do and don't carry moral weight. In Mangan's formulation of DDE, for example, the distinction carries moral weight only in the context of the other conditions he cites. For example, the proportionality condition is critical—it will not do to claim that an injury (or death) caused by a hot pursuit was merely foreseen but not intended if the reason for the initial intervention was something of minor significance (say, a misdemeanor moving violation).[12] Police should always be aware of the possible and foreseeable consequences of their acts, and especially if the tactics they employ are likely to have very harmful consequences.[13]

Attempts to say what it is about plausibly different cases, such that some are cases of morally permissible acts and others are not, do not always match the traditional intended/merely foreseen distinctions said to characterize DDE reasoning. Warren Quinn argues that what underlies the distinction between morally permissible and morally impermissible cases is a distinction between direct and indirect agency; that is,

> agency in which harm comes to some victims, at least in part, from the agent's deliberately involving them in something in order to further his purpose precisely by way of their being so involved (agency in which they figure as intentional objects), and harmful agency in which either nothing is in that way intended for the victims or what is so intended does not contribute to their harm.[14]

The distinction between direct and indirect agency, Quinn believes, provides whatever moral significance is possessed by the distinction between intended and merely foreseen harms but does not exactly correspond to the latter distinction. He believes, however, that the direct/indirect agency distinction expands what is traditionally seen as intended harm. As he says in a later article, "some cases of harming that the doctrine intuitively speaks against are arguably not cases of intentional harming, precisely because neither the harm itself (nor anything itself causally very close to it) is intended."[15] If Quinn is right about this, then an appeal to DDE will not work in cases of killing in self-defense.[16] A different principle will need to be invoked.

Conclusion

The Doctrine of Double Effect invites moral approval of intentional actions that have problematic side effects in cases in which those side effects are not themselves intended, and in which, they are foreseen and proportionate.

Although the doctrine is usually backed up by appeals to intuitively appealing examples, the intuitions are not universally shared, and it is not always clear whether there is a clear principle underlying such intuitions. It may well turn out to be the case that there is no single underlying principle, but that, insofar as such intuitions carry weight, various considerations might be appealed to. The issue is far from settled.

Notes

1. Thomas Aquinas, *Summa Theologica* (II-II, Qu. 64, Art. 7). From: *The Summa Theologiæ of St. Thomas Aquinas*, trans. Fathers of the English Dominican Province (Second and Revised Edition, 1920), available at: www.newadvent.org/summa/3064.htm#article7.
2. Joseph Mangan, "An Historical Analysis of the Principle of Double Effect," *Theological Studies* 10 (1949): 43. Whether there might be occasions in which the bad effect is intended as a means to bringing about a proportionately good end is not encompassed by the Doctrine of Double Effect and needs to be considered separately. See Chapter 10.
3. In general, see F.M. Kamm, *The Trolley Problem Mysteries*, ed. Eric Rakowski (New York: Oxford University Press, 2015).
4. One might argue that targeting the school will have the same political value as targeting the munitions dump.
5. Sherry F. Colb, "Excluding Illegally-Obtained Evidence and the Doctrine of Double Effect," *FindLaw*, 25/11/2009, available at: http://writ.news.findlaw.com/colb/20091125.html.
6. This debate is sometimes cast in terms of crime control vs. civil rights approaches. See Herbert L. Packer, *The Limits of the Criminal Sanction* (Stanford, CA: Stanford University Press). Those favoring the former wish to expand police powers in the cause of crime control, whereas those favoring the latter wish to curb police powers in the cause of civil rights—those of citizens generally, including suspected criminals.
7. Colb, "Excluding Illegally-Obtained Evidence and the Doctrine of Double Effect" (*emphasis in original*).
8. Ibid., (*emphasis in original*).
9. See Glanville Williams, *Criminal Law: The General Part* (London: Stevens & Sons, 1961); also "The *Mens Rea* for Murder: Leave It Alone," *Law Quarterly Review* 105 (1989): 387. See, generally, A.P. Simester, "Why Distinguish Intention from Foresight?," in *Harm and Culpability*, ed. A.P. Simester & A.T.H. Smith (Oxford: Oxford University Press, 1996), 71–102.
10. H.L.A. Hart, *Punishment and Responsibility* (Oxford: Oxford University Press, 1968).
11. John Stuart Mill, *On Liberty* (1863), ch. 1, para 11, available, inter alia, at: www.econlib.org/library/Mill/mlLbty1.html.
12. Police sometimes argue that if a person seeks to avoid apprehension in such cases, it is a sign that a much more serious offense is involved, thus justifying a dangerous pursuit. That, I think, is probably a rationalization.
13. In numerous cases, police officers or innocent motorists have been injured or killed when pursuing drivers who were using their cell phones. Certainly, cell phone use has been responsible for many accidents, but often unnecessary risk-taking on the part of police has been involved.

14. Warren Quinn, "Actions, Intentions, and Consequences: The Doctrine of Double Effect," *Philosophy and Public Affairs* 18, no. 4 (1989): 343.
15. Warren Quinn, "Reply to Boyle's Who Is Entitled to Double Effect?," *The Journal of Medicine and Philosophy* 16 (1991): 511.
16. Nor will it work in cases of self-sacrifice, as when a soldier throws himself on a hand grenade to save his fellows.

Chapter 7

Persons as Ends

> So act that you treat/use humanity, whether in your own person or in the person of any other, always at the same time as an end, never merely as a means.[1]

Thus reads the second formulation of Immanuel Kant's categorical imperative—what he argues to be the fundamental moral principle—often dubbed the Formula of Humanity. It raises many questions, only some of which we can address here. What is it about "humanity"? Why in one's own person as well as that of others? What is it to "treat" or "use" another? What is it to treat another as an "end"? What is it to treat another "merely" as a means? How are the two related?

The relevance of this formula to criminal justice in general and policing in particular should be clear. It reminds agents of the criminal justice system of the special status of those whom they encounter and engage with in their work. Whether such agents see their goal broadly as social peacekeeping or public safety, or more narrowly as law enforcement or crimefighting, they are to act toward other humans in a way that acknowledges or protects their status as "ends" and does not treat them as mere means to their own role-related (or other) ends. The formula is intended to hold not only for victims and bystanders, but also for their treatment of criminal suspects.

We will later consider in more detail what this involves in police-citizen encounters, though a useful cautionary tale is provided by a fairly recent Australian incident in which police ordered the drivers of several vehicles (including their passengers) to block a road on which a speeding driver was traveling.[2] Although the intention was to halt what turned out to be a 19-year-old learner driver in a stolen car, the driver did not stop but continued driving and plowed into the vehicles, causing injury and psychological damage to adults and children. Here police treated the car owners and passengers merely as means. A contrasting situation arises in the case of fleeing felons (or others)[3] who use hostages as human shields, ironically expecting police to treat them as ends.[4] In an example (to which we will return in

Chapter 8), a government agent, in order gain information about a criminal enterprise, began a romantic affair with an associate of one of the suspects, to the point at which the woman, believing the relationship to be genuine, became pregnant with the agent's child. However, once the agent gained whatever information he could, he "disappeared," leaving her shattered with the consequences of their "relationship."[5]

Although Kant's discussion of the formula is notoriously brief, he does have a few other things to say about it. For example, in *The Metaphysics of Morals*, he connects the idea of persons as ends with that of human dignity: "Humanity itself is a dignity; for a man cannot be used merely as a means by any other man (either by others or even by himself) but must always be used at the same time as an end."[6] And dignity itself is connected with rational autonomy understood as moral self-legislation: "the dignity of man consists precisely in his capacity to make universal law, although only on condition of being himself also subject to the laws he makes."[7]

As an illustration of the formula, Kant provides the example of a deceptive promise:

> he who has it in mind to make a false promise to others sees at once that he wants to make use of another human being *merely as a means*, without the other at the same time containing in himself the end. For, he whom I want to use for my purposes by such a promise cannot possibly agree to my way of behaving toward him, and so himself contain the end of this action.[8]

Whatever the obscurities in Kant's mode of expression, his assertions have usually been taken to capture something of intuitive moral importance in the way in which people should treat each other. People are not just objects to be used like knives and forks, or even expensive items such as cars, but warrant some special consideration that is grounded in something other than their monetary or social value. The challenge is to give an account of what it is that makes people different, along with its moral import.

Although Kantian scholarship is not here our primary concern, it is worth spending some time interpreting the Kantian formula. Initially, we should note two things about it: first, it does not state that people cannot ever be treated or used as means, only that they cannot be used *merely* as means; and second, although Kant appears to make the formula exceptionless or absolute, we might still want to defend its importance without seeing it as non-overridable.[9]

In looking at Kant's formula, perhaps the first point to note is the relatively minor one that not *every* engagement with others is a matter of treating or using them as a means to the furtherance of our own ends. If I say to my dinner companion, "Pass the salt," that, in and of itself, would not be considered a "use" of the other that is of moral interest. Let us consider why not. Robert Audi's distinction between using someone *merely* as a means and using someone *solely* as a means is of help here.[10] Suppose, in order to avoid having to eat alone at a restaurant, I invite a colleague to join me. My invitation is motivated solely to serve this end of mine. Am I treating my colleague merely as a means? Suppose that my colleague joins me for dinner and while we are eating, he gets a phone call from his wife telling him that his daughter has become ill and needs to be taken to a doctor. If I share my companion's concern and do not try to prevent him from leaving, even though it would frustrate my purpose in inviting him to join me (so that I would not be dining alone), then, though his presence was solely a means to the furtherance of *my* own ends, I do not treat my colleague *merely* as a means, for I also acknowledge him as an end in himself, with concerns and purposes of his own. My treatment of him is not exclusively as a means to my own ends.

The Kantian dictum is directed at the treatment of another person as a *mere* means. Let us look more closely at what this means. Suppose, wanting to know what hour it is, I notice someone with a watch and ask her what time it is. Does this make her a mere means to my end? My asking politely, my thanking her, my readiness to provide assistance if she trips as she reads her watch would show that I do not treat her merely as a means. No doubt, it is true that behind my politeness and even readiness to assist, there *could* be motivations that would disqualify me from fulfilling the Kantian dictum of always treating another as an end in him- or herself. Perhaps I view—as, no doubt, some people do—the use of politeness as simply social WD-40, employing it only as a means to get what I am after. This is certainly possible, and suggests that in determining whether someone is being treated (solely or merely) as a means, or as an end, it is not enough to look at the outward features of the actor's conduct. Context is everything here, as is specific background knowledge of the actors. Slicing into a person with a scalpel has a completely different meaning for Dr. Josef Mengele, a well-known Nazi physician who performed brutal research experiments on Jewish inmates in the Auschwitz concentration camp, and for a caring surgeon attempting to remove a patient's cancerous tumor so that the patient can continue to live comfortably. The attitudes and motivations of actors must figure into our account of whether those on whom they act are being treated by them, as means—solely or merely—or as ends in themselves. (Simply looking at what *A* does to *B* may sometimes give us some reason to think that *A* is, say, trying to rob *B*, but on closer examination, we may find that what *A* did was actually an innocent act, despite appearances to the contrary. The manner and motivation behind *A*'s actions need to be reviewed if we are to know the moral status of *A*'s conduct.[11])

Many cases can be presented that illustrate the point. For example, consider a salesman who pitches an expensive product to a customer, seemingly with the customer's interests and welfare at heart, but also with great indifference to the customer's ability to pay. Or take the case of police actions that cause injury to bystanders. Although the injury is not intended by the police, in responding to a situation that has the effect of causing injury to bystanders, the police may act with disregard for the status of these bystanders as persons who are ends in themselves. (Police are not always unknowing causes of such injury, but treat the harm to others as "collateral damage," damage that is unintended but acknowledged and even regarded as in some way justified.)

And then there are cases of what may be viewed as the "use" of others, but a use that is in no way incompatible with the regard of those others as ends in themselves. If, in order to shield myself from a strong wind, I move behind a group of people so as to lessen the impact of the wind upon myself, I use these people solely as a means. But in doing so, although I obviously do not treat these people *as* ends in themselves, it doesn't follow that my action is oblivious to their status as ends in themselves. Analogously, if I am being pursued and, to evade my pursuers, I dash into a crowd to "lose" myself, I use the people in question solely as means to my concealment. But, here too, it does not follow that using them in this way constitutes a disregard of them as persons who are ends in themselves. So, though these cases constitute the use of others as means, they do not constitute exceptions to what is at issue for Kant. What Kant has in mind is a certain treatment of others in which what I do impacts on their interests or abilities in a way that either disregards or undermines their interests.[12] We can see something of this in Kant's use of the case of the person who makes a false promise: the person to whom one makes a false promise is made to have false beliefs and expectations and, perhaps, to take actions or make plans in light of those beliefs and expectations. What we are doing when we make a false promise, then, is enlisting another person's interests to serve our own. (For this reason, Kant says that the person lied to "cannot contain in himself" the end of the person who is making the promise.)

Let us now turn to the question of what exactly it is that makes it morally wrong to treat another person as a means to our own ends.[13] Kant links the use of others as mere means to a denial of their dignity and he links human dignity to a person's "capacity to make universal law," adding, significantly, "although only on condition of being himself also subject to the laws he makes." No doubt, the idea of human dignity is itself ambiguous, with various writers interpreting it differently. Kant himself uses the term in more than one way, but what he says about human dignity that is most relevant to his claims of how human must be treated is his talk of the dignity of humanity as a noble rank that each and every human possesses.[14]

Although universal dignity (the dignity of humanity) is often associated with the human capacity for rational decision-making or autonomy,[15] I think Kant comes closer to the essential character of dignity when he links it to the human capacity for moral judgment. In Kant's words, "the capacity to make universal law" is a capacity that humans not only must recognize in others but also acknowledge in themselves. There is, thus, a status dimension to human dignity as well as a comportment or expressive one ("being himself also subject to the laws he makes"). As Kant puts it elsewhere, "morality is the condition under which alone a rational being can be an end in itself, since only through this is it possible to be a lawgiving member in the kingdom of ends. Hence morality, and humanity insofar as it is capable of morality, is that which alone has dignity."[16]

For Kant, our dignity resides in our status as normative beings whose moral decisions are not to be viewed by us simply in terms of means-end determinations, but as judgments of appropriateness and inappropriateness. It is our standing as moral agents (especially), given to evaluating courses of action as a condition for determining which courses are and are not to be pursued, that constitutes a critical element in our dignity. This process of normative reasoning gives a particular and special worth to what we do.

As well, Kant says that the capacity to make human universal law is constitutive of our human dignity only if those who exercise such capacity also see themselves as subject to the principles that they endorse. For Kant, then, there is more to human dignity than our capacity for certain kinds of decisional determinations. Such determinations must also be reflected in our own person. We must carry or comport ourselves in a certain way if we are to be creatures with dignity—as moral agents committed to the norms we articulate. Human dignity is not only a status; it also has an expressive dimension.

* * *

However, we should not jump to the conclusion that if we avoid treating others as mere means that we thereby treat them as ends. As Audi puts it: "merely instrumental treatment of persons might be conceived as a way of devaluing them. By contrast, our not treating them as ends, even when culpable, may indicate only failure to respect their value."[17] Note, however: there may be nothing wrong with treating others solely as means to ends of our own—many legitimate business and other formal transactions have this character. Although, as a customer, I may not treat the business people from whom I make a purchase as ends in themselves, I may still *nonculpably* treat them solely as a means. My treating them solely as a means might be culpable were I to fail to show sympathy or understanding in the event of a delaying accident on their part. (This is not to say that I should "accept" the delay. I may be in a hurry to get whatever I ordered, and it may be appropriate for me to cancel and then order from someone else.)

For Kant, we should not only avoid treating others as mere means but also positively treat them as ends. (As well, our transactions with others, especially when extended over time or conducted directly or face-to-face, should involve recognition of them as persons in their own right, and that means treating them as moral agents, as persons who are acting voluntarily, responsibly, and with feelings of their own.) We thus acknowledge their status as ends in themselves, an acknowledgment that can take various, even habitual, forms: looking directly at them, smiling, speaking politely, saying "please" and "thank you"—forms of expression, which, though they can be used mechanically, are, when sincere (even if habitual), expressive of a certain level of caring concern and sensitivity to others.

Clearly, there is more to treating other persons as ends than treating them well. And there is more to treating others well than saying nice things to them. "Buttering up" a person so that one may later defraud her is not treating her as an end, though for a time it may involve lavishing attention and gifts on her. The stories of lonely people seduced by the solicitousness of exploitative others indicates that treating others as ends is not merely a matter of acting toward them in certain ways but of doing so in a certain manner while being motivated to do so in certain ways. Those ways almost certainly include a care for the other's interests, including their interests as the other sees his or her interests.

One might wonder whether the exhortation to not only refrain from treating others merely as means but also to positively engage with others explicitly as ends is excessively demanding, especially given the frequency and (often) fleetingness of our many encounters with others—the bus conductor, the check-out person, the provider of forms in the government office, etc. Perhaps the key here is that, at the very least—and as Kant exhorts us—we always *regard* others as ends in themselves, even when circumstances are such that these others serve as means to our own ends. That is, even as we use others and they provide us with what we are seeking, there must always be a preparedness on our part to be responsive to these others' own personhood.

* * *

Consider again the implications for police work. A significant amount of that work involves conduct toward others—be those others inquirers, potential sources of information, victims, suspects, or simply bystanders present during some police activity. Police work tends to be very pragmatic, strongly goal oriented and, when the restoration and maintenance of social peace in populated areas is required, also quite demanding. In this context of diverse human activity—of multiple but distinct human needs and (often) pressing goals—there are judgment calls and exercises of discretion that provide multiple occasions for people to be treated, intentionally or not, as mere means to the accomplishment of tasks, and certainly occasions for failures to view others as ends in themselves. Police work involving crowd control, stop-question-and-frisk, questionings and arrests, interventions in public disputes, and dealing with critical incidents, all pose challenges for the way in which police conduct themselves and for the motivations governing both their involvement in each of these activities and how they go about their work. Moreover, the potential for less-than-acceptable interactions with others can be considerably exacerbated by the authority and power differentials that exist between police and those with whom they interact.

Our discussion of Kant and his views of human dignity is intended to remind us that those whom police encounter, whether as victims or perpetrators, possess a basic dignity by virtue of their being humans who have the capacity for moral judgments. We may not esteem those whose human dignity we must nevertheless recognize as placing a constraint on our actions toward them.[18]

As should now be clear, there are many ways in which police may violate the Kantian—or more general—moral expectation that people will not be used, abused, or have their dignity as persons ignored or violated. Consider again Kant's example of the person who makes a false promise. Suppose a police officer falsely promises a suspect that the suspect will get a probationary sentence if he confesses to a violent assault, though the officer knows that not only is such a promise not his to make, but also that such a confession is unlikely to result in only a probationary sentence. As Kant would see it, it would be irrational for the suspect to consent to what is being proposed as he desires an outcome different from what will *actually* transpire as a result of his taking up the officer's proposal. The false promise that is made to him is therefore degrading of him as a rational being with interests of his own.

If a suspect who flees is finally caught and subdued with physical force, the unnecessary punches and kicks, albeit fueled by an adrenaline rush, and even anger at the disrespect for authority that is shown by the flight, display scant regard for that person's humanity. Even use of "perp talk" (and use of the "perp walk") in a legal culture that professes innocence until guilt is proven is degrading.

Conclusion

Although the view that we should never treat others merely as means, but always as ends, is subject to a variety of interpretations, it has stood the test of time as capturing a general moral principle that should govern our human relations. In particular, it captures those elements of our being that are constitutive of our dignity. Within a pragmatic occupation such as police work, it has particular salience in police-citizen encounters, moderating what is often seen as a somewhat dehumanizing us-them relation in which the admirable ends of policing are tainted by disregard for the standing of others, even if they have acted badly and warrant intrusive police action.

Notes

1. Immanuel Kant, "Groundwork of the Metaphysics of Morals," in *Practical Philosophy*, trans. Mary Gregor (Cambridge: Cambridge University Press, 1996), 429. Sometimes "brauchst" is translated as "treat," sometimes as "use." The two are not

identical. One may treat a person in a certain way (say, contemptuously) without using them. http://platypus1917.org/wp-content/uploads/2011/07/kant_groundworkmetaphysicsmoralsbook.pdf.

2. "Police 'Used Human Shield of Vehicles' to Plug Up Road and Stop Stolen Car Speeding at 93mph," *Daily Mail*, May 17, 2012, available at: www.dailymail.co.uk/news/article-2145843/Police-used-human-shield-vehicles-plug-road-stop-stolen-car-speeding-93mph.html#ixzz1vAj93hTJ; Paul Millar, "Car Chase Outrage as Police Order Driver Roadblock," *The Age*, May 16, 2012, available at: www.theage.com.au/victoria/car-chase-outrage-as-police-order-driver-roadblock-20120515-1yp4t.html. Cf.
3. Kate Jacobson, "Witness Who Filmed Delray Melee Describes Chaotic Scene," *Sun Sentinel*, 12/31/2014, available at: www.sun-sentinel.com/local/palm-beach/delray-beach/fl-delray-melee-follo-20141231-story.html.
4. KOMO Staff, "Tacoma Cop Killer Shot Dead, Used Kids as Human Shields," *KOMONEWS*, 11/30/2016, available at: http://komonews.com/news/local/police-officer-shot-in-tacoma-taken-to-hospital.
5. See Gary Marx, "Under-the-Covers Undercover Investigations: Some Reflections on the State's Use of Sex and Deception in Law Enforcement," *Criminal Justice Ethics* 11, no. 1 (1992): 13–24. A 1999 revised version is available at: http://web.mit.edu/gtmarx/www/undercovers.html.
6. Kant. *Metaphysics of Morals/Doctrine of Virtue*, trans. Mary Gregor (Cambridge, UK: Cambridge University Press, 1991), 255, §38, Akad. 6: 462.
7. Kant. *Groundwork of the Metaphysics of Morals*, trans. H.J. Paton (New York: Harper & Row, 1956), §II, Akad. 4: 440.
8. *Groundwork of the Metaphysics of Morals*, trans. Mary Gregor, intro. Christine Korsgaard (Cambridge, 1998), Akad. 4: 429–30, available at: https://cpb-us-w2.wpmucdn.com/blog.nus.edu.sg/dist/c/1868/files/2012/12/Kant-Groundwork-ng0pby.pdf (*emphasis in original*).
9. It is at least a serious position that occasionally the consequences of not using someone merely as a means would be so massive that an exception could or should be made. This is sometimes argued in so-called "ticking bomb" scenarios in which torture is contemplated, or other scenarios in which innocents might be thought sacrificable for some general or greater good. We have already touched on this issue in the previous chapter, and will have occasion to return to it again.
10. Robert Audi, *Means, Ends, and Persons* (New York: Oxford University Press, 2016), 21–7. See also Samuel Kerstein, "Treating Others Merely as Means," *Utilitas* 21, no. 2 (2009): 163–80.
11. If one begins to treat someone merely as a means, this does not preclude a subsequent change of heart. One suspects that some relationships that begin in this way (a person viewed simply as a sex object) later evolve into relationships that are much deeper.
12. They need not be aware that their interests are being violated. This is often the case with privacy violations.
13. Though even that may be too fast: one may not treat another as a mere means without thereby treating that person as an end.
14. Historical precedents for the notion that all humans possess an inherent dignity and so must be treated accordingly can be found in Stoicism and Christianity. There are, of course, those who eschew any appeals to human dignity. The issues are discussed at greater length in John Kleinig and Nicholas Evans, "Human Flourishing, Human Dignity, and Human Rights," *Law and Philosophy* 32, no. 5 (September 2013): 539–64, from which I have borrowed.
15. In a more extensive discussion, we could draw various links to equality, given that dignity is possessed by all humans. Some of the connections are noted in Leslie

Meltzer Henry, "The Jurisprudence of Dignity," *University of Pennsylvania Law Review* 160 (2011): 207 n. 192.

16. Kant, *Groundwork*, 4: 435.
17. Audi, *Means, Ends, and Persons*, 70.
18. No doubt, there may be problematic cases, such as those involving psychopathy, in which apparent perpetrators' judgments seem to be severed from the *caring about* that should be associated with treating others as ends.

Chapter 8

Impermissible Means

> Laws are silent when arms are raised.[1]

As Cicero implied, when the stakes are high, means-to-valued-ends that we would otherwise reject may be tolerated. That, of course, is an observation, not a prescription or permission. May it also be (at least) a moral permission to use means to ends that we would otherwise reject?

It has certainly been thought so by some, even many. Over the years, Cicero's observation has frequently been invoked and interpreted as though it offered moral license for otherwise unacceptable means to the achievement of our goals. Prior to 9/11 (though with terrorism already acknowledged as on the rise), the late William Rehnquist, then Chief Justice of the US Supreme Court, wrote that "the laws will not be silent in time of war, but . . . they will speak with a somewhat different voice."[2] Rehnquist's carefully worded reflection on Cicero is not a denial so much as a qualification of Cicero's meaning. As Rehnquist understands it, in times of war, some civil liberties may need to be constrained, though he leaves it unclear how far such constraints may go. Do the sounds of war or threats of terrorism allow the detention of suspects without trial, the use of military tribunals, the warrantless interception of communications? Do they allow torture or torture-lite or interrogatory tactics that would otherwise be considered "cruel, inhuman, or degrading"?

A different gloss on Cicero was given in a British court case during World War II: "Amid the clash of arms, the laws are not silent, they may be changed, but they speak the same language in war as in peace."[3] This interpretation suggests that the laws may not speak with a normatively different voice, but that they may have to be re-framed to accommodate changed or wartime conditions. The implication is that the normative order will not be changed, even if situational considerations will need to be taken into account. If torture or third-degree tactics are generally forbidden on moral grounds, they will continue to be eschewed under wartime conditions.

The question we consider in this chapter is whether the adoption of some means to our ends is so problematic that they should be ruled out no matter how dire the circumstances. As we noted earlier (Chapter 3), the means we choose to pursue our ends may not gain all of their power simply by virtue of the ends that they serve, but can possess moral potency in their own right. Yet negative moral potency per se need not be enough to disqualify their use if the ends they serve are important or otherwise compelling enough. And so, as part of our security arrangements, we may regret having to search private backpacks and cases or having to ban the carriage of certain liquids aboard aircraft, but our determination of what is at stake—say, a terrorist attack exploiting those means—is important and probable enough to justify the compromise of certain freedoms. The prevention of terrorism is a very powerful social end.[4]

Important though the prevention of terrorist attacks is, we do not permit governmental authorities to intrude willy-nilly into every personal or private space. There were, for example, considerable and *legitimate* outcries against the use of airport body scanners that allowed for realistic images (showing genital areas or colostomy bags) rather than stylized captures of weapons concealed on passengers' bodies. Important though counter-terrorism measures were, there needed to be effective yet technologically less intrusive measures.[5]

Our main question here is whether some means—some techniques or strategies—are so problematic that they should not be used in *any* circumstances. This looks like a question about absolutism—whether there are some actions or practices that are absolutely forbidden in any and all circumstances—a source, for some, of comfort, though for others a sign of troubling and extreme dogmatism. Some years ago, British philosopher Elizabeth Anscombe published an influential article in which she was taken to be arguing *for* an intransigent, unyielding position regarding certain acts. She wrote:

> if someone really thinks, in advance, it is open to question whether such an action as procuring the judicial execution of the innocent should be quite excluded from consideration—I do not want to argue with him; he shows a corrupt mind.[6]

Anscombe's remark—and her paper in general—has often been interpreted as an assertion of absolutist dogmatism, but it is likely that a subtler and less contentious point is being made—namely, that some acts are morally problematic, no matter what the consequences, and any attempt to "neutralize" them, ahead of an assessment of the circumstances of their consideration, shows an egregious shallowness of moral understanding.

The issue I am concerned with here, however, is not whether, say, the wrongness of a particular kind of act (used as a means) is ultimately a matter of consequences, but whether, no matter what the consequences, certain kinds of acts should be prohibited. "Prohibited" here is ambiguous between morally rejected and institutionally prohibited. For example, someone might argue that although torture should be absolutely prohibited as a matter of *public* policy, circumstances can be envisaged in which it would be morally permissible. This is a tricky position to hold, because any morally permissible torture is likely to leach into an institutional defense exception even if torture is formally prohibited: once one instance of torture is judged morally permissible, efforts will be made to recognize exceptions to institutional bans.

Torture and Other Cruel, Inhuman, or Degrading Means

Torture is often held to be the quintessential case of a means that is absolutely wrong, though a similar judgment is sometimes made about certain means that, though one might not use the term "torture," are conveniently encompassed by the phrase, "cruel, inhuman, or degrading treatment."[7] These terms capture not only the kind of brutal treatment that we often associate with national security or wartime situations, but also the use of "third-degree" tactics by police to extract confessions from suspected criminals.[8] Although the use of third-degree tactics is now frowned upon as violating the voluntariness required for confessional evidence,[9] reports of their employment have not disappeared from the news,[10] and—as is often acknowledged in the use of "enhanced interrogational tactics" with respect to terrorists—sometimes the use of such tactics is implemented to extract information other than that which is germane to the evidence required for the purposes of conviction. This was the case in the kidnapping/ransoming in Germany of 11-year-old Jakob von Metzler. His kidnapper was apprehended, but the boy's whereabouts were not known, and it was feared that the child might be at imminent risk. To overcome the kidnapper's refusal to reveal the boy's whereabouts, Wolfgang Daschner, then Vice-President of the Frankfurt Police, indicated to the kidnapper that he would bring someone in who would torture the information out of him. Before the agent of torture arrived, however, the kidnapper relented and revealed the whereabouts of the boy (who, it turned out, had already been killed). Although Daschner's threat had powerful support, it was thought symbolically important to show formal disapproval. The Regional Court subsequently convicted him of ordering torture, of inducing the misuse of authority, and of coercion, and he was given a conditional fine and placed on probation.[11]

In determining whether torture or other forms of cruel, inhuman, and degrading treatment ought to be absolutely rejected, regardless of the objectives they are meant to serve, we must deal with a number of difficult questions: What is torture? How, if at all, should it be morally differentiated from, say, other forms of "cruel, inhuman, and degrading treatment"? Exactly what is it that makes torture wrong? Is what makes torture wrong sufficient to outlaw or condemn it in *all* circumstances? Or are there special configurations of circumstances that might legitimize or at least excuse the use of torture? What must we know about the circumstances that we appeal to in order for those circumstances to justify torture?

Some of these questions have been addressed, however inadequately, at a global (UN) level. Most member countries of the United Nations have signed and ratified the 1985 UN Convention Against Torture and Other Cruel, Inhuman, or Degrading Treatment or Punishment.[12] This Convention prohibits all uses of torture, making it clear that "no exceptional circumstances whatsoever, whether a state of war or a threat of war, internal political instability or any other public emergency, may be invoked as a justification of (state-sponsored) torture."[13] Superior orders are also rejected as a defense. The Convention characterizes torture as

> any act by which severe pain or suffering, whether physical or mental, is intentionally inflicted on a person for such purposes as obtaining from him or a third person information or a confession, punishing him for an act he or a third person has committed or is suspected of having committed, or intimidating or coercing him or a third person, or for any reason based on discrimination of any kind, when such pain or suffering is inflicted by or at the instigation of or with the consent or acquiescence of a public official or other person acting in an official capacity. It does not include pain or suffering arising only from, inherent in or incidental to lawful sanctions.[14]

Although there is no simple path from near universal agreement to absolutism, the fact of near-universal agreement should provide some defense against the claim that opposition to torture reflects a mere cultural (or "Western") convention.

Regrettably, quite apart from its restriction to those who act on behalf of the state, the Convention offers the kind of definition that has enabled countries such as the United States—supposedly "committed to the elimination of torture"[15]—to justify conduct that, under any commonsense understanding, clearly amounts to torture.[16] Part of the problem here lies with the word "torture" itself. Although it has philological roots in the idea of twisting and is associated with bodily writhing, physical mutilation, and graphic images of the rack and screw, the term was not always seen as designating a condemnable act, in the same way that the normatively charged act of murder is. Rather, the term was often used descriptively, such as "trial by ordeal," and torture was often employed in the service of justice—to gain confessions or impose judicially sanctioned punishment. For this reason, the term "torture," though it has tended to be linked most closely with very direct and painful physical invasions that distort the body, it was not until a few centuries ago (perhaps influenced by the Renaissance, and Enlightenment thought) that injury to the physical body was treated as injury to the self, the body now considered as deeply integral to our human selves.[17]

We should, in addition, not allow the traditional association with bodily assaults to distract our attention from the psychic dimensions of torture. Although the UN Convention explicitly covers mental pain or suffering, it is easy to think of such suffering only as that which accompanies some imposed physical invasions such as the application of electrodes to genitals or being forcibly kept in physically painful positions for hours at a time. What are we to say of the smearing of menstrual or of pigs' blood on the faces of devout Islamic detainees? Or of threatening reprisals against a detainee's close family members? Or even the injection of a so-called "truth serum" such as sodium pentathol?[18]

My own inclination here is to suggest that we focus less on whether particular invasions of another constitute torture and whether that should be absolutely—institutionally or morally—outlawed, and instead address the many ways in which we may subject those without the power to resist it[19] to cruel, inhuman, or degrading treatment. Then we should consider whether, and if so when, such treatment might be institutionally or morally acceptable. True, we must still consider what makes treatment cruel, inhuman, or degrading, but this way of engaging with the issue is likely to keep us focused on the normative (rather than merely definitional) considerations that underlie our concern with torture.[20]

Imposed suffering is *cruel* when it is deliberate and gratuitous. Such deliberate and gratuitous treatment violates a basic human requirement to respect the integrity of another. Torture does this by causing such suffering as to jeopardize the person's capacity to focus on anything but his or her pain and suffering, and the conditions for its alleviation.[21] The person is denied control over his or her own response to the world. Unlike the dentist's drill, it has no consensual purpose for the person who undergoes it.

Imposed suffering is *inhuman* when it manifests a disregard of what the humanity of others requires of us. Our fellow humans are, like we ourselves, creatures who exercise a certain agency or decision-making ability, one that is characterized by emotional and physical sensibilities, along with capacities for perception and reflection. Those who impose inhuman suffering on another subvert or trample on such requirements of interpersonal engagement, by seeking to eliminate the considered judgments and free agency of the other or by coercively exploiting those capacities in others to get from them what they would otherwise deny us. *Inhumane* treatment is treatment of another that is inappropriate for those who possess the sensibilities of a human being.

Imposed suffering is *degrading* when it violates the norms of human dignity. What human dignity consists of is a complicated and much debated issue, even though appeals to human dignity have become the cornerstone of most international human rights declarations, and in the Convention Against Torture, it is put forward as its basic moral resource.[22] My own view (outlined in the previous chapter) is that there are two parts to the idea of human dignity. One part refers to our capacity to be guided not only by reason, but also by moral considerations. One of our very distinctive human abilities is to see the world not simply as posing challenges to be met by whatever means we can use, but through a lens that distinguishes acceptable from unacceptable ways of achieving those ends. The other part of the idea of human dignity is constituted by our displaying that capacity for moral discernment in the way in which we go about living our lives. Degradation is a derogation from human dignity. We can, of course, degrade ourselves by casting aside the expectations that go with our capacity for virtue. But we can also degrade others by treating them in ways that threaten or cause them to give up the elements necessary to the exercise of their dignity. Reducing another human being to one who can no longer control his bodily functions, to one who can no longer guide his actions according to his best judgment, or to pitiful whimpering or begging, is to degrade that person, and we know from accounts of those who have been subjected to torture as well as to various "enhanced interrogation techniques" that they are often degraded in just those ways.

I think we may agree that some acts are more cruel, more inhuman, and more degrading than others. The question to consider is how best we are to make these differentiations. Is it by distinguishing certain graphic techniques from others or should we morally assess their differences by the way in which they derogate from human dignity and bear negatively on the ongoing life of the human person?[23]

The Ticking Bomb Argument

Much of the current debate about the legitimacy of (some) torture has revolved around what is called "the ticking bomb argument," a consequentialist argument of sorts that is designed to envisage circumstances under which torturous "cruel, inhuman, or degrading treatment" that might otherwise be seen as morally wrong (and so forbidden) would be morally permissible (or at least excusable). The argument maintains that however evil and however intrinsically evil some forms of torture might be, a case can be made for its infliction if the stakes are high enough. Ordinarily, the argument takes something of the following form:

> An evil scientist, Dr. Doom, has planted a nuclear device capable of devastating the whole of the New York City area. However, he and his devilish plot are discovered only after the device has been activated. It will explode within an hour and there is no way to evacuate the area in time. In such circumstances, would we not be justified in using

whatever means necessary—including torture—to get Dr. Doom to reveal the whereabouts of the device so that it can be deactivated?[24]

As presented, the argument is cast in terms of "justification" rather than some other normative category such as "permission," "something necessary but regrettable," or "sanctioned by a necessity that nevertheless leaves one's hands dirty." Each option has its defenders and its critics. Sometimes the argument is offered simply to show that there is a set of circumstances under which even the *most* cruel, inhuman, or degrading treatment could be morally sanctioned. At other times, the argument is offered as part of a slippery slope strategy—if the ticking bomb argument provides a clear-cut case for torture, then what circumstances less than a ticking bomb might also permit the use of cruel, inhuman, or degrading treatment? Or a different slippery slope is proposed: if it is somehow OK to torture Dr. Doom, then what about torturing Dr. Doom's wife or young daughter in the event that Dr. Doom is himself resistant but the prospect of seeing his wife or daughter tortured could get him to relent? Sometimes the strength of the argument is taken to show its weakness: if it takes an outlandish hypothetical, such as the ticking bomb, to show what would make torture permissible, then it is unlikely to find legitimate support in the real world.

In what follows, I shall look at certain aspects of the ticking bomb argument—or one of its variants—to indicate what I think is morally at stake at a particular point of the argument.

Perhaps the first thing to note about the ticking bomb argument (in the form just presented) is the high epistemic demands it makes. The argument presumes that we know—or at least have reason to believe with a high degree of probability—that (1) the threat *actually* exists, (2) it is as *serious* as it has been made out to be, (3) there is a *pressing* need for action, (4) *only* torture or something like it will succeed in getting the information needed to avert the threat, and (5) the threat is *very likely* to be averted as a result of the torture.

These are extremely high demands. We may easily enough specify what these demands are in an artificially constructed hypothetical case, but in a real-world situation, it would be extremely difficult to establish that these demands are met.[25] Even the fact that someone has claimed a ticking bomb exists is not enough—without a lot of supporting data—to indicate that it actually does. Most often—as was the case when (in the 1980s and 1990s) the Israelis were subjecting Palestinian detainees to what they termed "moderate physical pressure"—there was simply an environment in which serious terrorist attacks had occurred and there was some (albeit unclear) probability that a particular detainee would have information about a forthcoming attack. The ticking bomb argument also trades on the almost certainty of a massive amount of harm that would be caused should the bomb go off, and though some past North Korean rhetoric may make that more easily imaginable, the likelihood of that set of circumstances occurring is very small.[26] It is of course open to the argument's proponents to claim that a smaller cost (the damage caused by a "dirty bomb," for example) would still be sufficient to make the case. That is true, but it risks weakening the argument, which probably requires something enormous to be at stake in order to counter what may turn out to be diminished probabilities with respect to the other factors mentioned in the argument. The argument works cumulatively, and all its links need to be fairly strong. Even if a bomb has been put in place, how are we supposed to know with certainty that it is ticking and that time is of the essence—that is, that there is only enough time to defuse it, but not enough time to deploy other strategies that might have a greater probability of succeeding? One of the common complaints about the use of torture is that, despite the claims of its political proponents, it does not come with a very impressive track record.[27] Even if time is of the essence, and alternatives are limited, there is no guarantee that torture will yield critical information as effectively as other means of interrogation. In the example, if Dr. Doom is sufficiently committed to what he is doing, he may, when tortured, provide only false or delaying information.

As I mentioned earlier, the ticking bomb argument can be deployed to different ends. Its epistemic demands may be appealed to as a reason to resist any proposed use of torture. Or, if it is seen as offering a window for legitimate torture, it then generates a debate about limits. What if the number of lives threatened is not in the millions but only in the thousands or hundreds? Do we need 100% certainty that torturing Dr. Doom will force him to yield the information, or that, if we have the information, it will enable the bomb to be defused? And so on. Not all slippery slopes are unmanageable; however, given the variables in question (how much pain, and what kinds, how serious the threat, how likely the torture will be successful, etc.), working out a plausible judgment procedure will be very challenging.

Let us look again at what it is about torture (and its relatives) that makes it morally problematic.

The Wrongness of Torture

We've already associated torture with conduct that is in some way cruel, inhuman, or degrading. Insofar as torture is singled out for special attention, is that because there is something distinctively egregious about it, or is it that to call an act one of "torture" is to pick out treatment that is *especially* cruel, inhuman, or degrading—a difference in degree rather than a difference in kind? I'm inclined to think that the most plausible candidate for torture's distinctiveness—at least with respect to some instances of cruel, inhuman, or degrading treatment—is the fact that those who are made to suffer are placed under the complete control of those who inflict it on them, and so cannot resist the sustained assault on their persons. Moreover, those subjected to such treatment are almost never made privy to how far others will be willing to go in subjecting them to such treatment. Being held in ignorance of when their imposed suffering will end is part of the intended process of augmenting the torment and so breaking them down.

Not incidental to what is wrong with torture is the fact that torturers place their victims outside the moral community in that they are denied the opportunity to function as moral beings: they are reduced to objects for manipulation by others and made helpless to resist that manipulation. They are thus denied the basic moral concern to which all human beings have a right.

Unless we take the problematic position that those who are tortured do not reside within the moral community but are to be treated as non-accountable and even less than animals (whose torture is problematic enough), we must draw a moral line at cruel, inhuman, or degrading treatment. Such a line is to be drawn not only because of the regard that we should have for those tortured, but also because we who torture should be morally constrained from imposing such treatment on others.

"Assaults on the defenseless" occur not only in cases of unambiguous torture, but also in what is characterized as torture-lite. In my view, this is reason enough to undermine the drawing of any serious moral distinction between torture and many other cases of cruel, inhuman, and degrading treatment.

Some writers, such as David Sussman (referred to earlier), think that something else is distinctive about torture—namely, that it induces self-betrayal (or the threat thereof). One's own body is made into the enemy in that what is being done to it forces one, against one's will, to "go against" oneself and accede to the torturer's demands in, say, giving up information one doesn't want to divulge. However, since not all torture is for the purpose of extracting information from an unwilling person, I think it is best to see in torture and its relatives just the imposition of certain kinds of cruel, inhuman, or degrading treatment on those who are denied the resources for resisting it.

If we have a lively sense of what it is about cruel, inhuman, or degrading treatment that makes such treatment so unconscionable, then we will be in a better position to understand moral resistance to the conclusion of ticking-bomb-like arguments. Even if we think that the ticking bomb argument offers us a limiting case in which torture would be permissible, it will help us to understand why we should be ever vigilant about—and resistant to—expanding its scope to accommodate those seeking greater flexibility in their fight against terrorism. We should always be acutely sensitive to the fact that those who appeal to ticking bomb scenarios typically do not wish to restrict their justifications to the conditions outlined in the argument itself, but see appeal to the argument as a way of opening the door to additional cases in which torture or other forms of cruel, inhuman, or degrading treatment might be imposed. It is partly the recognition of this that makes it so important to draw out the many underlying epistemic assumptions on which the argument relies. Our experience of the frequent misapplication—and even corruption—of authoritative license when it comes to approving the torture of others should warn us against such openings. If someone resorts to torture on ticking bomb grounds, and we are sufficiently persuaded and perhaps even moved by the details of a particular case, we may—perhaps—forgive or excuse that person's resort to torture in *that* particular instance, but we should never allow or countenance "advance directives" for the use of torture.[28]

No doubt, even torture admits of degrees in terms of the suffering caused, the degree of degradation, and the likelihood of long-term effects on the person tortured.[29] But we need always to avoid nearing the point at which harsh measures cut into the humanity and dignity of another, the point at which the moral agency of that person is denied—because the capacity for judgment has been overtaken by the imposed suffering.[30] If there are rare occasions when torture seems the only option—perhaps a father trying to get information about the whereabouts of his small and at-imminent-risk children—resort to torture will still leave its considerable moral stain on the person who authorizes it and on the person who engages in it.[31]

Conclusion

Deliberately subjecting defenseless others to cruel, inhuman, or degrading treatment not only degrades those who do it, but also the society that is willing to tolerate it, for it indicates a willingness to reduce human beings to a state that denies their (capacity for) moral agency. No society that has moral standing should countenance this. Rather, in the name of whatever purpose—punishment, retribution, the gathering of information, etc.—for which it is undertaken, the intrusion into the personhood of another that torture represents should be condemned absolutely.

Notes

1. *Silent enim leges inter arma*: M. Tulli Ciceronis (c. 106–43 BCE), *Pro T. Annio Milone ad iudices oratio*, intro. and comm. Albert C. Clark (Oxford: Clarendon, 1985), 10.
2. William H. Rehnquist, *All the Laws But One: Civil Liberties in Wartime* (New York: Alfred A. Knopf, 1998), 221.
3. Lord Atkin, *Liversidge v. Anderson* (1941), 2 All E.R. 612.
4. Whether terrorism is always an end to be eschewed is something that I simply assume here. A more focused study would need to establish that in the face of certain defenses that have been offered. See, e.g., Virginia Held (ed.), *How Terrorism Is Wrong: Morality and Political Violence* (Oxford: Oxford University Press, 2008). At the same time, we should also be aware of the ways in which concern for "national security" can be corrupted for political advantage.
5. See the discussion in John Kleinig, Seumas Miller, Peter Mameli, Douglas Salane, and Adina Schwartz, *Security and Privacy: Global Standards for Ethical Identity Management*

in Contemporary Liberal Democratic Societies (Canberra: ANU E Press, 2011), 97–100, available at: http://epress.anu.edu.au?p=162481.

6. G.E.M. Anscombe, "Modern Moral Philosophy," *Philosophy* 33 (1958): 17.
7. Although presented as alternatives, treatment that fails on one of these counts often fails on the others.
8. Other possibilities include the use of certain kinds of sexual exploitation by police undercover investigators. See the references to Gary Marx's work in Chapter 7, fn. 5.
9. Jerome H. Skolnick and James J. Fyfe, *Above the Law: Police and the Excessive Use of Force* (New York: Simon & Schuster, 1993), ch. 3.
10. For a recent report, see Jason Meisner, "City Agrees to Pay $9.3 Million for Wrongful Conviction Tied to Burge Detectives," *Chicago Tribune*, 1/10/2018, available at: www.chicagotribune.com/news/local/breaking/ct-met-wrongful-conviction-jon-burge-20180110-story.html.
11. See "Police Threat Fuels Debate on Torture," available at: www.dw-world.de/dw/article/0,,785751,00.html; BBC News, "German Officer Guilty of Threats," available at: http://news.bbc.co.uk/2/hi/europe/4111483.stm. An extended description of the case is provided in Paul Nieuwenburg, "Is There Such a Thing as Government Ethics? Or: A Machiavellian Plea for Excuses," available at: http://soc.kuleuven.be/io/ethics/paper/Paper%20WS1_pdf/Paul%20Nieuwenburg.pdf.
12. See: https://en.wikipedia.org/wiki/United_Nations_Convention_against_Torture#/media/File:CAT_members.svg.
13. UN Convention Against Torture and Other Cruel, Inhuman, or Degrading Treatment or Punishment (1985), art 2.1.
14. Art. 1.1.
15. Cf. the comment of then US President George W. Bush: "The United States is committed to the worldwide elimination of torture and we are leading this fight by example," *Statement on United Nations International Day in Support of Victims of Torture*, June 26, 2003, available at: www.presidency.ucsb.edu/ws/index.php?pid=294.
16. See Karen J. Greenberg and Joshua L. Dratel (eds.), *The Torture Papers: The Road to Abu Ghraib* (New York: Oxford University Press, 2005).
17. In Platonic thought, the body was thought of as the wayward container of an immortal soul. On the elevation of cruelty, see Judith Shklar's discussion of Montaigne (1533–1592) in *Ordinary Vices* (Cambridge, MA: Harvard/Belknap, 1984), ch. 1: "Putting Cruelty First."
18. See Linda M. Keller, "Is Truth Serum Torture?," *American University International Law Review* 20 (2005): 521–612.
19. It is a critical feature of torture that those who are tortured are in no position to resist (see Henry Shue, "Torture," *Philosophy & Public Affairs* 7 (1977–78): 130). The victim is deprived of resources to resist what is being inflicted on him or her.
20. I have attempted to spell out my concerns in more detail in John Kleinig, *Have We Become Too Fixated on Torture?* Pamphlet issued by Association for Services to Torture and Trauma Survivors (ASeTTS), lecture given on the occasion of the UN International Day for the Support of Victims of Torture, June 26, 2008, available at: www.asetts.org.au/Documents/HaveWeBecomeTooFixatedonTorture.pdf.
21. David Sussman goes further, to suggest that—at least in interrogatory torture—the victim's body is used as an agent of self-betrayal, so that the torture victim thereafter feels alienated from his body, "What is Wrong with Torture?," *Philosophy & Public Affairs* 33, no. 1 (2005): 1–33. But though that way of looking at torture may illuminate something about the devastation that torture often causes, it may be no less applicable to cases of torture-lite, in which a person's body or deepest self may also be exploited to cry out against him or her to accede to the interrogator's demands. It is not simple physical pain that makes certain techniques so destructive, but the psychological impact that they have, and this can be brought about through threats

and other psychologically invasive practices no less than through direct physical interventions.

22. Preamble to the UN Convention.
23. We should not forget that so-called torture-lite techniques are often used cumulatively, and this magnifies their potency. See Metin Başoğlu, Maria Livanou, and Cvetana Crnobarić, "Torture vs Other, Cruel, Inhuman, and Degrading Treatment: Is the Distinction Real or Apparent?" *Archives of General Psychiatry* 64 (March 2007): 277–85.
24. There are many versions of the argument. The earliest version of which I am aware is found in Jeremy Bentham's essay "On Torture" (written during the period 1777–1779, but unpublished during his lifetime). An edited version is published in W.L. Twining and P.E. Twining, "Bentham on Torture," *Northern Ireland Legal Quarterly* 24 (1973): 307–56. Bentham treats torture as a neutral category, its justifiability or otherwise being a function of its overall utility.
25. See the attempt to construct such a case in the film *Unthinkable* (Sony, 2010).
26. It is important to the argument that the consequences of failing to torture are serious enough to make the old maxim "let justice be done, though the heavens fall" appear to be a *reductio ad absurdum* rather than a reasonable statement of principle.
27. Darius M. Rejali, *Torture and Democracy* (Princeton, NJ: Princeton University Press, 2005), ch. 21; Ali H. Soufan, *The Black Banners: Inside the Hunt for Al-Qaeda* (New York: Penguin, 2011).
28. Although I am suggesting a stronger moral case against torture, there is an interesting and related jurisprudential discussion about the defense of "necessity," which, if successful, functions to justify what would otherwise be prohibited. But an important element in that discussion is the recognition that the defense of necessity must be considered on a case-by-case basis.
29. See, for example, the grisly options described in W. Krousher Richard (pseud.; Tony DeBlase), *Physical Interrogation Techniques* (Port Townsend, WA: Loompanics Unlimited, 1985).
30. So-called torture-lite can have as serious long-term psychic effects as unvarnished torture: Jessica Wolfendale, "The Myth of 'Torture Lite'," *Ethics and International Affairs* 23, no. 1 (2009): 47–61; though see David Sussman, "'Torture Lite': A Response," same issue, 63–7. See also, R. Bellaby, "Torture-Lite: An Ethical Middle Ground?" *International Journal of Applied Philosophy* 29, no. 2 (2015): 177–90.
31. We will have more to say about "dirty hands" in Chapter 10.

Chapter 9

Other Problematic Means

> For my part, I think it a less evil that some criminals should escape than that the Government should play an ignoble part.[1]

Thus opined US Supreme Court Justice Oliver Wendell Holmes, Jr. when dissenting in *Olmstead v. US*. Roy Olmstead was part of a large bootlegging operation during the Prohibition years (1920–1933), an operation exposed using wiretaps that had received no judicial approval. Although the US Supreme Court at the time held that the evidence gathered violated neither the Fourth nor Fifth Amendments, that decision was later overturned in 1967 by *Katz v. US*.[2] Justice Holmes was prescient in arguing (in 1928) that it is better for government agents to act nobly than to secure convictions, even of the guilty. Even valuable ends are better forfeited than realized by means that are "ignoble."

I have already argued that ends, good though they may be, do not ipso facto justify the use of whatever means may secure them. Justice Holmes appreciated this, and his opinion is captured in the strictures for which I argued in Chapter 6. My argument there was that means must meet certain moral bars if they are to give ethical sanction to governmental (including police) efforts to secure criminal justice ends.

In the present chapter, we shall focus on one particular social value that needs to be especially protected when law enforcement agents move to realize desirable ends. That value is social or institutional trust. It is my contention that trust is a central social value, one that is easily compromised and lost and, when lost, restored only with difficulty. Threatened by crime and other socially disruptive activities trust, once lost, must be restored and then preserved by the agents of criminal justice, who must always be careful to act in ways that promote and preserve trust.

Let us look at the nature and importance of trust.

Individual, Social, and Institutional Trust[3]

Individual, social, and institutional trust are all closely related, each varying only in its scope. Early liberal writers, Locke among them, argued for the importance of social and institutional trust. Locke argued that humans, though concerned with personal security and the advancement of their own personal interests, are naturally social creatures, whose hopes and plans for themselves include many activities that depend on the involvement and cooperation of others. But the pre-civil state of nature is also home to flawed human beings, and though the integration of their activities is supposedly governed by the rational deployment of their rights, the ungoverned operation of their choices results in a social environment of considerable insecurity and distrust. The outcome, a decision to enter into civil society governed by enforced rules and regulations, is an attempt to shore up the failures of trust in a state of nature and to re-establish it within human communities. Civil society both requires and promotes trust among its members. We trust the institutions of society to do their job of justly regulating civil life; in turn, that regulation inspires reasonable expectations and trust in us that, so long as we ourselves behave according to reasonably imposed civil strictures, we can trust others to do so, as well. That the institutions of civil society are thus based on our trust in others abiding by the laws of those institutions, and others doing so, reinforces our trust in those institutions as providing reasonable insurance against social uncertainty and insecurity.

Of what does trust consist? Paradigmatically, trust is interpersonal—*A* trusts *B*, where *B* may be an individual, collective, or a human institution (such as a government, a judiciary, or a police department). When we speak of trust in nonhuman objects—such as vehicles, resources, or appliances (*F*)—that sort of trust is best understood as a *reliance* on those objects, the common feature here being an expectation or confidence that the object of trust or reliance will deliver what we expect of it (Ø). *A* trusts *B* to Ø or relies on *F* to Ø, where Ø generally ranges over a limited number of activities or operations. A difference between them, however, is that in trusting another human being (or institution), one makes oneself vulnerable to betrayal of that trust, whereas in relying on something, one merely opens oneself to possible disappointment. It bears noting that the vulnerability to betrayal involved in trusting another need not assume that one's trust was "blind." Blind trust *is* a form of trust, but it is not a paradigmatic (or even perhaps an especially desirable) one. Trust may, and usually ought to, be warranted, the warrant being based on what one knows, or has reason to know, about those whom we trust—namely, that they are *trustworthy*.[4]

Trust tends to reflect the relationship we have with the person or institution that we trust, whereas reliance reflects merely the degree of confidence we have in something being the way we think it is. *A* may rely on her dictionary or chainsaw without trusting it. Insofar as relations among people are concerned, person *A* may not trust individual or institution *B*, but may nevertheless rely on *B* to do something because *A* may have a high degree of confidence that *B* will do that thing while recognizing that *B*'s doing or not doing that thing will not be on account of anything having to do with *B*'s relationship to *A*. The point is not that trust lacks an epistemic component, but that, paradigmatically, trust bespeaks the character of a relationship.[5]

The trustworthiness of persons and/or institutions is a function of several factors, including their *competence* to secure what is expected by the person who trusts, as well, of course, as *a will* (or commitment) to provide it. Those whom we trust must see themselves as normatively expected to do what it is trusted that they will do. Though no more than this may be necessary, frequently, the trust we have in others presumes their *care* for, or *goodwill* toward, us. This is not to gainsay that persons who take their role seriously or institutions that take their role seriously may be completely trustworthy without caring for those who are served. Their care may be for performing their role well, rather than for those whom their role is intended to serve.

Just as trust may range from completely warranted to totally blind, it may also be associated with various degrees of confidence. Trust may sometimes involve little more than a hope or intuition that the object of trust will deliver. (Sometimes we may have little choice but to trust—or at least hope—that some person or institution will do what is needed.) On the other hand, an overconcern with the warrantedness of trust may display a lack of trust. Parents who won't trust their children until they have shown themselves to be trustworthy may find that their offspring do not develop traits of trustworthiness (or, indeed, of being trusting). Governments or police departments that are constantly called upon to demonstrate their goodwill and competence may find reciprocal lack of trust. As the vulnerability requirement indicates, trust involves risk, but not all risk is unjustified. Judging when trust is justified and when not is one of the great challenges of trust.

No doubt, the warrantedness of trust will depend significantly on the circumstances under which it is to be exercised. I may reasonably trust a stranger to give me the correct time, but not to mind my wallet. I may reasonably expect a police officer to give me accurate directions, but not to give me sophisticated financial advice.

When we are not in a position to know whether a particular person or institution is trustworthy for a particular purpose we may rely on third-party warrants to assist us. This is the function of "Good Housekeeping" seals, as well as of service training certificates and academic and professional certifications. All of these help to mediate between those who need to trust others (of whose competence and reliability they are unsure) and those who are trusted (or entrusted) to carry out certain duties and/or provide sought-after goods and services. Of course, such third-party assurances are not guarantees of trustworthiness, but they offer some epistemic basis and so some warrant for trust that what one needs to be done will be done.

In addition to a certain degree of trust being essential to the smooth functioning of social and institutional life, trust is integral to many intimate, valued, and valuable interpersonal relationships. A friendship without trust would hardly qualify as friendship (and a social order without trust among its members would cease to be a social *order*).[6] Indeed, some level of trust must be assumed by those who engage in any interpersonal and institutional activities. And this is so whether or not the relationship or institution is held to be of general positive ethical value, for trust is also integral to relationships—personal and institutional—when those relationships do not serve morally benign ends (though they still have value to those who are party to them). Trust may shape the bonds of solidarity and attachment among gang members, members of militias, and organized-crime families. It does not follow from this that trust lacks normative content, only that it can be misplaced. The members of the gang or corrupt institution may have good warrants for the trust that they place in each other, even though the associative relation is itself ethically problematic (and may be known to its members to be so). The mere fact of trust does not sanctify a relationship. Wider values also impact on the value we accord it. Even friendship, one of the great goods of human life, may be perverted by the core commitments that undergird it: a fellowship of greed or hate.

Apart from its intrinsic value to human relationships, trust may also have considerable instrumental value, for it may serve as a necessary condition for various types of social action. Social action may be highly varied and is critical to our development and flourishing. Indeed, many of the social enterprises in which we as individuals engage can be achieved *only* if others are trusted to do certain things and act in certain ways—to produce edible food, manufacture safe supplies and instruments, sustain reliable communications networks, provide security in a dangerous or precarious social environment, and so on. In addition, much human action is also joint—running a business or school; participating in a team or orchestra; fighting crime and ameliorating social disorder; human nurture; and research. Moreover, the acquisition of knowledge and even the attainment of a degree of personal autonomy are goods that would be unachievable were we unable to trust others' activities, as well as, to some degree, others' goodwill. We would not be the persons we are were there not significant trust among people and in social institutions. Indeed, much that is threatening to human well-being can be recognized as emanating from distrust—or, ironically, to our misplaced trust in untrustworthy others. It is not simply that we are what we are by virtue of our trust-relations with individual and collective others, but that our achievements as persons are not only enabled but also encouraged by a human climate of trust. What is referred to as warranted or justified trust is valuable, both in itself and for what it enables.[7]

Are there any generalizations that we can endorse about those persons and/or institutions in which we should put our trust? Is there a general answer to the question of what warrants our trust? One might be inclined to argue that, between people or people and institutions, trust should be the default position, needing support only where there is some reason to doubt the trustworthiness of the other. At a base level, there is probably something to be said for that. Nevertheless, it falls seriously short of what we know about human fallibility and frailty. Not only do we—and the institutions to which we are beholden—lack competence in many areas, but we and they are also frequently self-interested in ways that would betray any trust that might be placed in us or them. Even if we begin our lives in trust, we must subsequently learn when to trust, when not to trust, and when to distrust—not only other individuals but also social and institutional groups as well.

When we say that trust is warranted, we do not mean—paradoxically—that we have reasons for trust that do away with the need for it. Even if we did mean that, we would probably not have reason to do away with it, because the reasons we invoke to "replace" the need for trust are themselves likely to be erected on a foundation of trust—trust in the integrity of the research of others, for example. In talking about the warrantedness of *A*'s trusting *B* with respect to Ø, we are not denying that there are reasons for such trust; we are denying only that the reasons are of a kind that would undermine trust. Such reasons may be important if one is to accomplish some end or maintain some relationship. If, for example, I am asked by police to vacate a particular area, it may be advisable for me to trust the demand. This does not necessarily rule out my asking why, but it is likely to limit the extent to which I engage in a further process of questioning. It may diminish our trust in police if we later find out that their request had no legitimate public safety rationale. Similarly, if I wish to remain in a friendship, then it is strategically advisable that I do not keep questioning whatever the friend says—not that all questioning is ruled out. Gullibility is trust that has broken free from warrantedness.

Given the connection between trust and trustworthiness, the warrantedness of trust will depend first and foremost on the reasonableness of deeming some person, group, agency, or institution to be trustworthy. This will involve an assessment of the other's competence and the other's commitment to provide the Ø that is the point of the trust. Given that police are more likely to fail as a result of incompetence than ill will, failures in competence may impact trust as much as failures in goodwill. Not that goodwill is unimportant. As noted earlier, along with the importance of judgments of competence to trustworthiness, there may also be judgments about the extent to which the object of the trust cares for or bears goodwill toward one.[8] Even though trust may be warranted on the basis of an assessment of the other's competence and commitment, sometimes one may want more. We want not only a commitment to provide Ø, but also a commitment to *B* and *B*'s interests. This need not be interpreted as *A*'s adopting *B*'s interests as *A*'s own, but may include *A*'s willingness that *B* advance his or her own interests. This helps to explain why many failures of trust are experienced as serious betrayals and not just as disappointments. We may of course learn that the failure was due to circumstances over which the other had no control; but where it arises from some choice of the other, the failure is likely to be keenly felt.

Even if the other chose—quite reasonably—to give priority to some more demanding obligation, we have reason to expect an apology for the breach of trust. Police, for example, will often have competing obligations, and the investigation of misdemeanors may lose out to the investigation of serious crimes. However, given that we have vested in police the requirement that they take breaches of the law seriously, there should be at least some mechanism whereby triaging prioritizations can be rationalized.

A person's or institution's trustworthiness may also depend on larger social factors that bear on the relationship between *A* and *B*. Critical theorists have sometimes insisted that if a society is closed (homogeneous) or ideologically skewed (beholden to narrow ideologies) or financially impoverished, a good deal of what is standardly deemed "knowledge" will reflect censorship or dogma or will be otherwise lacking in relevant competence. *B* may be "socially formed" by certain broad views that qualify the commitment or goodwill that she may have to *A*. Indeed, some societies are more conducive to warranted trusting individual and institutional relationships than others, and the extent to which trust in others should be a default position may depend significantly on larger social factors that are more deeply social than personal.[9]

Trust and the Means of Policing

Our somewhat extended discussion of trust—individual, social, and institutional—has been intended to focus on a dynamic that is critical to police/community relations—albeit one that is often marked by the lack, rather than the presence, of trust. Vesting in police the various social prerogatives and discretionary powers they have—prerogatives to use force, to engage in deception, to invade privacy, and, more generally, to exercise discretion in how they go about their work—itself requires a substantial commitment of trust on the part of the community they serve. If police powers are incompetently used or are abused—if police unnecessarily or disproportionately use force, use deception, invade privacy, or use their discretion unwisely—community trust will be jeopardized, and their legitimacy will be called into question. Moreover, the community's cooperation—cooperation that the police need in order successfully to carry out their duties—will be forfeited.

In the past—and even now—many excesses and misjudgments in the use of police prerogatives have had a negative impact on the trust between police and their communities. Reports of these excesses have included the shooting of unarmed (particularly black) men, unnecessary and unwarranted stop-question-and-frisk practices, disproportionate stops of black men in moving vehicles ("Driving While Black"), and even disrespectful language. These and other ill-judged uses of coercive police authority have often reflected social and racial discrimination, which have contributed to and reinforced a lack of trust between police, people of color, and the larger community. Both at a national level, as well as in more localized contexts, unwarranted surveillance by police (whether or not judicially sanctioned) has contributed to suspicion that our privacy is of relatively little value to those entrusted with our safety. Furthermore, the realization that lying and deceptive practices by police (either as part of their investigations or during their interrogations) have become routine has deeply influenced the level of cooperation that citizens are prepared to give police. Finally, poor discretionary judgments on the part of police have contributed to a loss of trust in the professionalism that citizens expect of those to whom important social powers are given.

Part of the problem of sustaining the trust of the community in police has been the lack of transparency in their work. Although there will always be situations in which an ongoing investigation needs to have limits set on the availability of information, all too often police conceal what might reasonably be available for public scrutiny, and, too often, police have given an account of a police-citizen encounter that has had to be revised in the face of further scrutiny, later discovery, or—nowadays—a videorecording of the incident. Concerns about the lack of transparency (and the accountability associated with it) are beginning to be addressed. The growing prevalence, and transformative significance, of videotaping is such that many police departments are now requiring officers to wear body cameras so that there is an ongoing record of police-citizen encounters. Insofar as they offer a fuller and more graphic representation of such encounters, recordings on police body cameras may benefit officers as well as citizens by deterring (or providing evidence of) merely vexatious complaints.

Tellingly, the body-camera initiative has so far been only an imperfect remedy for the lack of police transparency. Trust is a function of the confidence that police and citizens have in each other, and is not something amenable to a simple technological remedy. Body cameras are not always turned on or are said to malfunction; police departments are often reluctant to make videotape recordings available to the public, or make them available only after accountability decisions have already been made. Moreover, in the absence of a sound track, even the best videotape recordings are limited in the information that they can provide, and may require considerable interpretation for a coherent and persuasive story to emerge. At this point, community concern about the lack of transparency in police work and the associated lack of accountability has yet to be fully addressed. What the use (and misuse) of body cameras by police reminds us of is that trust is a function of the confidence that the community and police have in each other; lack of trust is not amenable to a simple technological remedy. To be sure, the use of body cameras may serve as a constraint on the sort of behavior that erodes trust. But, as indicated earlier, trust is a social relationship in which parties show mutual respect and even goodwill in the effort to safeguard mutually shared ends. If it turns out that body cameras (or other devices) lead to greater truthfulness in the reporting of police-citizen encounters, and so to more appropriate responses, they will also contribute to a social environment in which trust is better able to flourish.

It is frequently noted that operational police officers have a considerable amount of discretion in their encounters with citizens, albeit a discretion that is diminished or must be structured in certain ways if the issues are serious (if, for example, a felony crime appears to be involved). How that discretion is handled is a matter of professionalism. Professionalism is about good judgment, and good judgment is a matter of discernment and decision-making that is based on considerations that are reasonably judged to be relevant to the issue at hand. Professionalism does not require perfection, but insofar as police have been given the authority to make judgments on behalf of the rest of us, we expect that their training and impulses will lead to significantly better decision-making than we could exercise on our own.

Conclusion

Because we vest in police considerable authority to act on our behalf, especially in matters of security, public safety, and social order, we permit them to act in ways that would otherwise be seen as problematic. They may use coercive force, engage in deception, infringe privacy rights, and use their professional discretion in their interactions with others. To be sure, the use of discretion, especially in relation to others' rights, is not unconstrained. Police are constrained by what we would be permitted to do on our own behalf (or on the behalf of others) in a state of nature. That constraint is important to the trust that sustains police authority. So long as we are able to see police as trustworthy, as acting in ways that we could and would agree to, then their use of force, the employment of deceptive tactics, the infringements of privacy, and their discretionary decision-making will be seen as acceptable. Of course, we will not get, nor should we expect, universal acceptance of all that police do, for not only will some have no interest in police fulfilling their assigned role, even for those who do have such interest, there may be disagreements about both their role and the way they go about fulfilling it. However, so long as what police do can be reviewed by the people they serve—without discriminatory divisions—we will have the resources we need for keeping our trust.

Notes

1. Oliver Wendell Holmes, Jr., *Olmstead v. US*, 277 US 438, 470 (1928) (in dissent).
2. 389 US 347 (1967).
3. Much of what follows is based on my "Trust and Critical Thinking," *Educational Philosophy and Theory* 50, no. 2 (2017): 133–43.
4. Ø may be very specific (that *B* will keep a particular appointment or political promise) or more generalized (that *B* will be transparent or honest with *A*). Even where no Ø

is specified, there will be conventional or implicit understandings about the scope of the trust.

5. May *A* trust *B* but not rely on *B*? I can think of circumstances in which a person might say: "As much as I trust *B*, I cannot rely on him (or it)." The assertion of trust expresses a confidence in *B*'s good will; the lack of reliance may indicate *B*'s lack of competence or reliability. Normally, though, even blind trust will also imply reliance, albeit unwarranted.
6. The Hobbesian expectation was that life outside civil society would be "solitary, poor, nasty, brutish, and short" (*Leviathan* [1651], ch. 12). Locke was a little less pessimistic, but also believed that the state of nature was no place for reasonable people to live out their lives.
7. This is not to deny that the inherent or instrumental value of the trust may be overridden or negated by the associative relation in which it is embedded.
8. A corollary to the importance of trust is the importance of trustworthiness. Being trustworthy can be very demanding.
9. George Orwell, *Nineteen Eighty-Four* (London: Secker & Warburg, 1949), dramatically illustrates the point.

Chapter 10

Dirty Hands and Noble Cause Corruption

> How you cling to your purity, young man! How afraid you are to soil your hands! All right, stay pure! What good will it do? Why did you join us? Purity is an idea for a yogi or a monk. You intellectuals and bourgeois anarchists use it as a pretext for doing nothing. To do nothing, to remain motionless, arms at your sides, wearing kid gloves. Well, I have dirty hands. Right up to the elbows. I've plunged them in filth and blood. But what do you hope? Do you think you can govern innocently?[1]

With these contemptuous words, the old revolutionary, Hoederer, censures the idealistic Hugo, who wants to be part of the revolution while demurring over the use of morally suspect though admittedly effective means. Jean-Paul Sartre's 1948 play *Les mains sales* (*Dirty Hands*), which echoes themes we encountered earlier in the discussion of Trotsky and revolutionary morality (Chapter 3), presents a fairly stark contrast between utility and morality. It has its policing exemplar in Dirty Harry, Clint Eastwood's eponymous police hero.[2] Harry gets things done—too bad if the methods sometimes cross moral lines, and institutional/constitutional constraints are flouted. Ultimately, the ends of the good guys are served: people are saved, and/or crooks pay their social debts.

The dirty hands/Dirty Harry phenomenon reflects, albeit somewhat crudely, a longstanding debate in political thinking. Much of it is traceable to the Florentine politician Niccolò Machiavelli, whose fame (or notoriety) is often said to lie in his advocacy of an amoral *Realpolitik* of the kind that Hoederer exemplifies. Of central importance to Machiavelli's most famous work, *The Prince*, a manual for rulership, is the advice: "It is necessary for a prince wishing to hold his own to know how to do wrong, and to make use of it or not according to necessity."[3] However, Machiavelli's wording suggests that a subtler message is being conveyed. The prince has a responsibility to secure his domain and legacy and, as desirable as it might be that he do so in a manner conforming to the precepts of morality, situations are likely to arise in which observing those precepts would be destructive to the fulfillment of his responsibility. A wise prince will need to be alert to circumstances in which wrongdoing is called for. This is not the thought of a person who is unmindful of what morality decrees, nor is it the thought of a person who has no regard for moral constraints. Rather, as Machiavelli writes, the prince must learn "how to do wrong."[4]

Some centuries later, though still prior to Sartre, the sociologist Max Weber famously distinguished two modes of governing—one by means of an "ethic of responsibility" (*Verantwortungsethik*), the other by means of an "ethic of principled conviction" (*Gesinnungsethik*). In the former case, legitimate political decision-making requires that desirable ends take into account the effects of means used to achieve them, even if on occasion doing so pushes one in the direction of moral compromise. In the latter case, the moral purity of one's ends or intentions is deemed to be overriding, and the consequences of their pursuit morally irrelevant. Weber associates this perspective with a strand of Christian thinking in which one does what is right "and places the outcome in God's hands."[5] Although Weber is careful to note that the former approach does not involve a simple utilitarian calculus and that the latter approach is not simply irresponsible, he believes that *those who govern* should favor an ethic of responsibility. He does not believe that the two approaches can be reconciled. He allows, nevertheless, that situations may arise in which the compromise involved is *too* great, and the morally responsible role occupant must stand on principle: here I stand, I can do no other.[6]

A more recent advocate of some willingness for moral compromise is Michael Walzer, who used the Sartrean metaphor in his influential 1971 essay "Political Action: The Problem of Dirty Hands." There he argued that those who enter public life sometimes must not only be prepared to dirty their hands, but ought to do so.[7] One of Walzer's examples is that of a reform-oriented candidate who, in order to get electoral support, must make a corrupt deal with a dishonest ward boss. Another example Walzer appeals to in order to buttress his view parallels the "ticking bomb" argument that we discussed in Chapter 8. Like Machiavelli, Weber, and Sartre, Walzer believes that there is some moral sanction for dirtying one's hands. Dirtying one's hands is, he says, sometimes the "right" or "justified" thing to do, at least in "utilitarian terms." The latter qualification indicates Walzer's moral unease. Morality is not just about utility, and Walzer is troubled by the moral compromise that it sometimes creates. Much of his article is therefore concerned with articulating an appropriate response to those who dirty their hands. Should we view their action as heroic (should they succeed in their effort to secure important ends), as tragic (insofar as they have sacrificed their souls),[8] or as having discharged a responsibility (that must nevertheless be expiated)? Walzer argues for the last of these options.

The issue of dirty hands most often arises as a consequence of having to act on behalf of others in some official role. It is claimed that those who hold public office will sometimes find themselves in situations such that they can fulfill the public expectations of their office (and so do what is in the public good) only if they act in ways that transgress ordinary moral expectations. The transgressions may range from lies to betrayals. The restriction to official roles is not strictly necessary (as we will see), though it meshes neatly with situations that may arise in a law enforcement context. In the case of police, it is precisely the fulfillment of their public role that is said to sanction the occasional dirtying of their hands.

The dirty hands debate entered the domain of law enforcement ethics via Clint Eastwood's 1971 film *Dirty Harry* (and Carl Klockars' influential critique),[9] but a distinct law enforcement version of the issue has perpetuated itself as "noble cause corruption." This term was introduced in Edwin Delattre's *Character and Cops* in 1989, and quickly found a place in subsequent police ethics discussions.[10] More than "dirty hands," the phrase "noble cause corruption" captures the tension created when the demands of public office (the noble cause) conflict with those of ordinary morality (leading to what is termed "corruption"). Given their social and professional roles and duties, police are almost certain to encounter situations in which competing normative demands invite corruption for a noble cause.

Nevertheless, a central confusion has infected much of the "dirty hands"/"noble cause corruption" discussion, at least in the criminal justice context. It is common for writers to conflate "dirty hands" with "noble cause corruption," seeing one as equivalent to the other. But a review of the literature suggests that there are striking differences, not least in the fact that whereas dirty hands theorists generally suggest that it is sometimes right or permissible or best or legitimate to dirty one's hands, there are very few who openly support "noble cause corruption," whatever the case might be *sotto voce* on the part of police practitioners. This suggests—correctly, I believe—that there are subtleties and nuances in this area that need to be brought out.

These nuances are embedded in Edwin Delattre's original discussion of "noble cause corruption." In line with his concern with character, it is Delattre's view that what is referred to as noble cause corruption is linked to two moral defects that may be manifested when a hard decision is to be made: arrogance and cowardice.[11] Both those who arrogantly believe that their ends (say, getting "undesirables" off the streets) always justify or excuse their means, *and* those who cowardly withdraw from making hard decisions while remaining in office, act corruptly.[12]

Naïve pragmatism, in which the ends are taken to justify the means, is at the heart of noble cause corruption, and is the reason it is almost always condemned. Testilying (lying under oath or in court) to ensure the conviction of someone one believes to be guilty (or at least a public nuisance), falsifying confessions, flaking (the manipulation or planting of evidence), and various constitutional "shortcuts" purportedly taken under the color of law are typical of such noble cause corruption.

Clearly, cases vary, and are known to vary in different ways, and this may account for the support for "noble-cause corruption" that is to be found among police, and, perhaps especially, those police who see their job as public safety or the pursuit of justice. Not every regulatory constraint on police procedure on every occasion mirrors an articulable moral constraint, and situations arise in which police officers consider respect for procedural rules an unnecessary hindrance to the legitimate cause of justice. If a police officer is asked whether he managed to keep someone he was pursuing "in sight at all times," he may consider it irrelevant that the person in question rounded a corner and hid behind a shed, or that he knew for sure that what the person threw into the bushes (and was later recovered) was a handgun. Police will be inclined to be more categorical than they might and sometimes ought to be. The world does not come to us neatly packaged, and there will be a spectrum of cases in which police will testify with confidence, in order not to have any uncertainties exploited, lest the "guilty" be able to escape justice.[13]

The dangers inherent in such uncertainty are clear enough, and not easily reduced to bright-line rules, though the history of what has passed for noble cause corruption is cause for understanding its abuses, as well as its attractions.

By way of contrast with such cases, a person who has struggled with the moral quandary into which the human condition has cast him, and has done the very best he can to make the right decision, cannot reasonably be charged with corruption. That situation, and the decision it requires, comes close to what Walzer (following Machiavelli and Weber) refers to as a "dirty hands" one.

Sometimes (as Delattre recognizes), we are confronted with having to make tragic or wretched decisions and, although Delattre is properly troubled by the ways in which this possibility can be and sometimes is abusively exploited, he does not think that we should pretend that decisions are easier or more clear-cut than they are.[14] Although not a case in which a public official must make a decision involving a clash between moral demands and the expectations of office, the awful case that is central to William Styron's *Sophie's Choice* captures the moral dilemma well.[15] Here the clash is between the demands of a more private role (motherhood) and the demands of morality. Following her transportation to a Nazi concentration camp with her two young children, Sophie is ordered by a Nazi officer to choose which one of her two children she will keep and which will be killed, warning her that if she refuses to make a choice both will be killed. Whatever choice Sophie makes, she will be left with a horrible moral burden. She will be left, it is said, with dirty hands, a residue of guilt for the choice she has made. For her (the novelist's character), the moral burden eventually becomes an unbearable psychological burden.

Most dirty hands situations arise in the context of a clash between the moral burdens of a role (sometimes public, sometimes more private) and the ordinary (universal) demands of morality. It is, in other words, a clash within a moral framework rather than one between a moral and non-moral one. Just because public servants occupy roles that require a special regard for public good, they may find themselves in situations in which they must choose between a large-scale public failure and the failure to honor important moral obligations to particular others. In the case of a politician or police officer, it will be a tension between the moral demands of office (to serve the general welfare and/or to maintain public safety) and acting so as to respect other human beings and do what we owe to them. True, in many cases we have already carved out for ourselves a range of exceptions (prioritizations) that apply to role performances or institutions. Thus, we ordinarily permit police officers to use force or deception to the extent that it would be permissible for us were we in a state of nature.[16] These allowances should not be viewed as "dirty hands" situations so much as acknowledged exceptions to well-known and non-absolute rules. But in the case of dirty hands, we are not dealing with conventional exceptions to rules, but rather with decisions that, even if correct, leave a "moral residue" on one's hands.[17]

Dirty hands situations are not all of a piece, and our responses to them cannot be rendered formulaically.[18] On many occasions, they arise as a result of the immoral acts of others. It was not Sophie who created her moral dilemma, but the Nazi officer who presented her with an impossible choice. Not long after the events of 9/11, questions arose about what a government official should do were it made known to him or her that a terrorist-commandeered commercial air flight was headed for a strategic center, such as the Capitol building in Washington, D.C., into which it would then crash. Would it be permissible to authorize the shooting down of the plane, despite the inevitable deaths of its innocent passengers that that it would cause? Or should one oppose a strategy that would certainly cost so many innocent lives even though that might be the *only* way to avert the high-jackers' intended devastation of the Capitol and the innocent lives that might be caused by *that* destruction?[19] Any government official faced with having to make such a terrible decision is in the unenviable position of having to choose between two options, neither of which will allow either clean hands or a clear conscience.

Not all cases of dirty hands involve such diabolical choices. Some years ago, when flash flooding in New Jersey stretched local police services to their limit, a police officer who lived in an affected area sought permission to assist his family. It was denied and, after the officer left (without permission) to attend to his family's needs, he was fired for insubordination. Clearly, in the police department for which he worked, his role obligations were deemed to take precedence over his family obligations.[20] More was at stake in a famous wartime case, in which British officials chose not to warn the people of Coventry of an impending air raid by the Germans lest it alert the German military to the fact that the British had cracked the Enigma Code that the Germans used for secret communications and in which the impending raid on Coventry was recorded.[21] In this case, maintaining the secrecy of the military advantage over the enemy (of having successfully deciphered its military code) was deemed more important than were the lives of Coventry's residents (whose protection could have been secured only by warning them of the impending raid, and so alerting the enemy that its military code had been broken). Deciding what to do in this case had to have been fraught in the extreme, given that the military advantage whose protection was at stake was seen to be an advantage that would (at least eventually) translate into the saving of many innocent British lives. Since a decision in *either* direction would result in the saving of some innocent lives and the sacrifice of others, any official(s) responsible for making the fateful decision would, *either way*, unfortunately, be left and so burdened by, dirty hands.

Granted that dirty hands situations may be our unavoidable lot, what kinds of considerations should enter into our decisions about what to do? Some considerations may be procedural, others substantive. One procedural consideration, suggested by Delattre, is that the decision in such a situation be one that is made only by the most authoritative person available in the circumstances. In a hierarchical organization such as policing, in which one presumes that rank correlates reasonably well with experience and maturity of judgment, this makes a great deal of sense and so is a suggestion well taken. Delattre also suggests that, as a precautionary measure, departments draw their own regulatory boundaries a bit tighter than may be required by social or legal norms, for this shifts the onus onto those who must make decisions in morally choppy waters. A third procedural suggestion is that decisions be made only on a case-by-case basis. This is entirely reasonable, if we take seriously Machiavelli's view that a prince's decision whether or not to do wrong be made "according to necessity." Although not identical to necessity in law (where necessity is treated as justificatory), political necessity, like necessity in law, should not be established by predetermined rules but on a case-by-case basis.

Among the substantive considerations that one should take into account is the *seriousness* of the violation that will be involved. Some breaches will ordinarily be minor breaches of regulations that organize deployments, for example, confining one's work sphere to geographical sectors. Crime does not confine itself to sectorial divisions, and officers may sometimes find it more efficient to treat them as guidelines rather than rules. (However, it may involve fudged paperwork.) At the other end of the spectrum, a decision, say, to jeopardize the lives of innocents may create a serious moral dilemma. A hostage taker who uses an innocent person as a shield, while threatening others, may present police with a decisional nightmare. Where the violation will affect others, one substantive issue might focus on the *identity of the violated*. Dirty Harry's violation of the urban terrorist Scorpio's constitutional rights might be seen to mitigate the wrong that he perpetrates in the name of justice. Or, consider the complex situation that is developed in the 2010 thriller *Unthinkable*, when the plausibility of the terrorist Yusuf's claim to have planted nuclear bombs in three cities is assessed and used to "justify" his torture.[22] Or, when it is realized that Yusuf has anticipated such torture and is unlikely, under torture or the threat of torture, to be persuaded to reveal the whereabouts of the three planted bombs, and attention shifts to Yusuf's young children and it is threatened that they, too, will be tortured if Yusuf does not reveal the information. Yusuf relents, but the lead interrogator is convinced that there is a fourth bomb, and demands that the children be brought in again. Whatever one might think about the legitimacy of torturing Yusuf—even that may be wrong—the "unthinkable" act of torturing his children is clearly more problematic, morally speaking.

Other substantive considerations will reflect factors that we discussed (in Chapter 5) when we reviewed what needs to be taken into account when contemplating the means we choose to employ in relation to the ends we choose to pursue via those means. Prominent among those factors are (1) how likely it is that the means chosen will actually serve the "noble cause" we aim to serve, (2) the importance and nature of the public good that is sought to be accomplished, and (3) the likelihood of undesirable externalities.

Ultimately, as has been emphasized on a number of occasions, the various factors will need to be brought together for judgment rather than calculation.

Conclusion

Although noble cause corruption is often—and often rightly—condemned as an example of amoral pragmatism, with its naïve appeal to ends to justify the use of means, there is clearly a wide spectrum of cases to be dealt with. In some of these cases, operational police may see themselves as legitimately cutting corners in order to secure what they judge to be worthwhile ends. Although these decisions might not always rise to the level of the dirty hands situations envisaged by Walzer and Delattre, they belong in a gray area that police will oftentimes feel they occupy, and an oversimplified "noble cause corruption" will assert its claims.

As a dimension of their professionalism, it is important for police to learn how to articulate the reasons behind the decisions they make in a way that addresses and satisfies the concerns of those likely to be affected by those decisions. That is fundamental to the legitimacy of their acting on our behalf.

Notes

1. Jean-Paul Sartre, *No Exit, and Three Other Plays*, trans. Lionel Abel (New York: Vintage, 1958).
2. *Dirty Harry* (Warner Bros, 1971), *Magnum Force* (1973), *The Enforcer* (1975), *Sudden Impact* (1983), and *The Dead Pool* (1988).
3. Niccolò Machiavelli, *The Prince*, trans. W.K. Marriott (1513/1532; Stilwell, KS: Digireads.com Publishing 2005), ch. 15, 57, available at: www.gutenberg.org/files/1232/1232-h/1232-h.htm#link2HCH0015.

4. Ibid.
5. Max Weber, "The Profession and Vocation of Politics" (1919), trans. and reprinted in *Weber: Political Writings*, ed. Peter Lassman and Ronald Speirs (Cambridge: Cambridge University Press, 1994), 359.
6. Weber quotes the words without attribution (367). Traditionally they have been attributed to Martin Luther when summoned before the Diet of Worms, though the exact words appear not to be Luther's.
7. Michael Walzer, "Political Action: The Problem of Dirty Hands," *Philosophy & Public Affairs* 2, no. 2 (1973): 160–80.
8. Or, as Weber puts it, following an ethic of responsibility endangers the "salvation of the soul" (366).
9. Carl Klockars, "The Dirty Harry Problem," *Annals of the American Academy of Political and Social Science* 452 (November 1980): 33–47.
10. Edwin A. Delattre, *Character and Cops: Ethics in Policing*, sixth ed. 2011 (Washington, DC: AEI Press, 1989), ch. 12. For something of the history, see John Kleinig, "Rethinking Noble Cause Corruption," *International Journal of Police Science & Management* 4, no. 4 (2002): 287–314; Seumas Miller, *Institutional Corruption: A Study in Applied Philosophy* (Cambridge, UK: Cambridge University Press, 2017), ch. 4. Some writers see the criminal justice discussion as part of a much wider-ranging problematic, that of "task-related rule breaking." See Robin Christiaan van Halderen, "Noble Cause Corruption Revisited: Toward a Structured Research Approach," *Public Integrity* 19, no. 3 (2017): 274–93.
11. Delattre, *Character and Cops*, 211–12.
12. Very little attention is paid to the indecision of the latter group.
13. I have offered several such cases in Kleinig, "Rethinking Noble Cause Corruption."
14. Assuming, of course, that the struggle is not made a cloak for self-deception, a possibility of which Delattre is acutely aware (personal communication, June 18, 2002).
15. William Styron, *Sophie's Choice* (New York: Random House, 1979). Film (1982) and opera (2002) versions have followed.
16. Unlike us, however, police are obligated to intervene in situations from which, as individuals, we might turn away.
17. The phrase was introduced by Bernard Williams, "Ethical Consistency," *Proceedings of the Aristotelian Society* 39 (1965, Supplement): 103–24. For a recent discussion see Lisa Tessman, *Moral Failure: On the Impossible Demands of Morality* (New York: Oxford University Press, 2015), ch. 2.
18. See, for example, Kenneth I. Winston, "Necessity and Choice in Politics: Varieties of Dirty Hands," in *Professional Ethics and Social Responsibility*, ed. Daniel E. Wueste (Lanham, MD: Rowman & Littlefield, 1994), 37–66.
19. For an extended discussion, see Tziporah Kasachkoff and John Kleinig, "Civil Emergencies and the Claims of Innocence," in *Shooting to Kill: Socio-Legal Perspectives on the Use of Lethal Force*, ed. Simon Bronitt, Miriam Gani, and Saskia Hufnagel (Oxford: Hart Publishing, 2012), ch. 2, 19–46. Reputedly, President George W. Bush's Vice-President, Dick Cheney, advocated such a position. See Dana Milbank, "Cheney Authorized Shooting Down Airplanes," *Washington Post*, June 18, 2004, A01, available at: http://www.washingtonpost.com/wp-dyn/articles/A50745-2004Jun17.html.
20. See Anon., "Police Officer Faces Dismissal for Loyalty to Family in Storm," *New York Times*, 9/29/1987, A2, available at: www.nytimes.com/1987/09/29/us/police-officer-faces-dismissal-for-loyalty-to-family-in-storm.html. Not all police departments have taken the same view. Some have provided for precedence to be given to familial obligations.
21. See R.V. Jones, *Most Secret War: British Scientific Intelligence 1939–45* (London: Hamish Hamilton, 1978).
22. *Unthinkable* (2010), extended version.

Concluding Note

When I began this project—of exploring means-end justifications in the context of police work—I wasn't too sure how it would turn out. At the time I conceived of it, the topics seem to have been made for each other, as policing is strongly ends-oriented, and many of the ethical problems that confront police arise out of the means that are used to secure their ends. I think that perception was basically correct, though I was often reminded how multi-layered police decision-making is, and of how that makes for a complexity in their decision-making that I sometimes side-stepped. Police are answerable not only to the citizens with whom they are in immediate contact, but also to wider public expectations, their fellow officers on the street as well as within the police hierarchy, to mayors and politicians, to prosecutors and defense lawyers, and of course to their own personal world views and these often create complications for concrete decision-making that warrants a much more detailed discussion than I often provided. Ranking such ends is something that does not lend itself easily to formulaic resolution and may be partly a matter of individual judgment. As well, others may have different ends and be willing to countenance a different slate of means, or even have a different perception of the use that a particular means may have. To have sought to unravel and work through these complexities would effectively have turned the book into a single complex case study—not necessarily a bad thing, but not how I originally conceived it.[1]

That said, the dialectic of means and ends pervades police work, and the unfinished business of providing a persuasive account of that dialectical interplay lurks behind much of what police are expected to provide decisive responses to in their daily work. My task, as I saw it, was to shine some light on the relationship between the two, to cast a good deal of police ethics as a particular way of seeing that interaction, and—from my own disciplinary perspective—to offer a somewhat novel way of linking ethical police decision-making with an old and ongoing debate in ethics. Others will judge how well I have succeeded.

At the same time, I have been conscious that practical reason, as a philosophical focus, and particularly the means-end reasoning that tends to be central to if not exhaustive of it, remains contested and messy, and that the lens I was proposing to use to consider some important aspects of police work was hardly a well-polished one. In the end, the desire to keep the discussion close to policing, or at least to practical examples, meant that many of the theoretical issues in practical reasoning that philosophers find interesting were too remote from my focus. The literature on practical reasoning is much more detailed and abstract than is useful for the practicalities of police ethics, and my discussion gives a good deal of that literature short shrift.[2] For example, I give very little attention to the theoretical issue of motivation in practical reasoning—how we get from reason to practice (connected to what philosophers often like to characterize as the debate between externalism and internalism)—and I concentrate almost exclusively on some of the issues that arise for operational police: what we determine to be relevant to action and the pursuit of ends. True, attitudes and intentions arise at this level, but it is still a trek from here to the issue whether reasons for action are themselves motivating, and, if so, how. Hume's famous challenge—"Reason is, and ought only to be the slave of the passions, and can never pretend to any other office than to serve and obey them"[3]—is left unconsidered.

It is, nevertheless, my hope that this extended essay on ends and means has emphasized the importance of considering each for ethical decision-making.

Many discussions of moral reasoning make some reference to what is often referred to as a publicity test—whether the decisions that one makes can be sustained in a public forum. This test is not a criterion of correctness, but points to the importance of scrutinizing one's decision-making—of seeing how others might question what one decides and whether one has the rational resources to meet/address those questions. The somewhat pragmatic account of justification that I provide in Chapter 5 attempts to be responsive to this consideration, and my discussion will have served one of its main purposes if it helps to achieve that openness to public scrutiny that should characterize police accountability in a liberal democratic society.

Notes

1. A fairly successful case study of this kind can be found in Vidar Halvorsen's unpublished doctoral dissertation, *Ethics, Force and Violence in Policing* (University of Oslo, Acta Humaniora, 2001).
2. For an overview, see R. Jay Wallace, "Practical Reason," *The Stanford Encyclopedia of Philosophy*, Spring 2018 ed., ed. Edward N. Zalta, available at: https://plato.stanford.edu/archives/spr2018/entries/practical-reason/.
3. David Hume, *A Treatise of Human Nature* (1739–40), bk. III, part 3, §ii.

Index